THE
PHILADELPHIA
CHEF'S TABLE

2ND EDITION

THE PHILADELPHIA CHEF'S TABLE

EXTRAORDINARY RECIPES FROM THE CITY OF BROTHERLY LOVE

2ND EDITION

ADAM ERACE & APRIL WHITE

Globe
Pequot

Guilford, Connecticut

*Restaurants and chefs often come and go, and menus are ever-changing.
We recommend you call ahead to obtain current information before
visiting any of the establishments in this book.*

Globe
Pequot

An imprint of The Rowman & Littlefield Publishing Group, Inc.
4501 Forbes Blvd., Ste. 200
Lanham, MD 20706
www.rowman.com

Distributed by NATIONAL BOOK NETWORK

British Library Cataloguing in Publication Information Available

Library of Congress Cataloging-in-Publication Data Available

ISBN 978-1-4930-4070-4 (hardback)
ISBN 978-1-4930-4071-1 (e-book)

♾™ The paper used in this publication meets the minimum requirements
of American National Standard for Information Sciences—Permanence of
Paper for Printed Library Materials, ANSI/NISO Z39.48-1992.

contents

Introduction | ix

Starters & Snacks | 1

Friday Saturday Sunday | 3
Oysters with Frozen Meyer Lemon
    Mignonette

K'Far | 5
Kale & Feta Borekas

Barbuzzo | 9
Whipped Ricotta with Grilled
    French Table Bread
Bruschetta with Stracciatella &
    Fava Beans

Sampan | 13
Sweet Shrimp with Radish &
    Citrus Salad
Beef Lettuce Cups with Tomato
    Salad

Distrito | 17
Veracruz Ceviche

Bistrot La Minette | 21
Oeuf du Pêcheur

Alma de Cuba | 24
Empanada de Verde with Onion
    Confit & Artichoke Escabeche

In the Valley | 27
Smoked Trout Mousse on
    Pumpernickel Toast

Vernick Food & Drink | 31
Uni with Warm Scrambled Eggs &
    Whipped Yogurt

Soups & Salads | 35

Vedge | 36
Chilled Cucumber-Avocado Soup
    with Smoked Pumpkin Seeds
Hearts of Palm, Beach Style

Oyster House | 39
Oyster Stew
New England Clam Chowder

Rouge | 42
Bibb & Endive Salad

Parc | 45
Salade Lyonnaise

Tria | 49
Grilled Asparagus Salad

Kanella Grill | 52
Watermelon Salad with Feta &
    Almonds

Poi Dog | 54
Chicken Long Rice with Scallions
    and Crispy Chicken Skin

Pastas | 57

Fork | 58
Suckling Pork Tortellini

Zeppoli | 61
Gnocculi all'Argentiera

Vetri | 63
Spaghetti with Green Tomatoes &
    Razor Clams

Morimoto | 66
Soba Carbonara

Buddakan | 69
Edamame Ravioli

Talula's Garden | 71
Potato Gnocchi with Mushrooms
    & Egg

Melograno | 74
Carbonara al Profumo di Tartufo
    Bianco e Acciughe
Testaroli al Pesto di Asparagi

Han Dynasty | 77
Dan Dan Noodles

Entrees | 81

Osteria | 82
Pork Milanese with Arugula Salad

El Rey | 85
Chile en Nogada

Zahav | 89
Chicken Freekeh
Whole Roasted Lamb Shoulder
    with Pomegranate

Amada | 93
Paella Valenciana

Good Dog Bar | 96
Roquefort-Stuffed Burger

Standard Tap | 99
Chicken Pot Pie

Pumpkin | 103
Stout-Braised Short Ribs with
    Maitake Mushrooms

Paesano's Philly Style | 107
Lasagna Bolognese

The Dandelion | 109
Fish & Chips with Tartar Sauce

Sabrina's Cafe | 112
Smoked Salmon Eggs Benedict
    with Home Fries
Pumpkin Pancakes

Bibou | 117
Roasted Duck with Potato Crique
    & Asparagus

N. 3rd | 119
Asian-Spiced Tuna Burger

**Booker's Restaurant &
Bar** | 123
Fried Jerk Chicken & Waffles with
    Pineapple Butter

Hungry Pigeon | 127
Chicken Sausage, Egg & Cheese
  Breakfast Sandwiches

Hardena | 131
Yellow Curry with Egg & Tofu

Lalo | 135
Lechon Kawali with Garlic Fried
  Rice and Tomato Salad

South Philly Barbacoa | 138
Chicken Mole Tortas

Townsend | 141
Cote de Boeuf for Two with
  Basquaise Panzanella

Desserts | 147

Franklin Fountain | 148
Hot Fudge Sundae

Honey's Sit n' Eat | 151
Carrot-Pecan Cake with Maple-
  Cream Cheese Icing

Lolita | 155
Cheesecake with Cajeta Caramel

Suraya | 159
Rose & Pistachio Cruller

Terrain Garden Cafe | 162
Blackberry Elderflower Tart with
  Lemon Poppy Ice Cream
Tomato & Ricotta Gelati with Basil
  Seed Pudding

Index | 167

About the Authors | 171

INTRODUCTION

Anthony Bourdain famously said in the 2012 episode of *The Layover* he filmed in Philadelphia, "There will be no cheesesteaks." Many of us Philly locals loved him for that. We were in the breathless throes of the restaurant scene's Third Wave, and as a snapshot of the best and brightest at a very specific time—screw the stereotypes—it worked.

Given the choice, I don't want to write about cheesesteaks. I don't even want to eat them, unless they're from Mike's BBQ and loaded with fat-slicked petals of smoked brisket. But you can't discuss the Philly food scene writ large without bringing the sandwich up. First, the Philly-has-nothing-but-cheesesteaks argument became national cliché. Then the evolving wisdom of "Philly has *so much more* than cheesesteaks," which the national media picked up as a talking point around the time Steve Cook and Michael Solomonov opened Zahav in 2008, went into such heavy rotation, it became its own cliché.

"With each bite, the whole country is discovering what Philadelphia diners have known for more than a decade," April White, the author of the first edition *Philadelphia Chef's Table*, wrote in 2012. "Beneath the neon and swagger of our signature street food, the City of Cheez Whiz has grown into a bona fide food destination."

From the Restaurant Renaissance of the 1970s through the Starr-Vetri-Garces-Turney Revolution of the early aughts to the post-Third Wave water we've been treading, one way or another we've had to contend with three ingredients (bread, beef, cheese)—four if you're doing onions. Like it or not, the cheesesteak is something that's defined us, and something we've used as a foil against which to define ourselves, for decades.

Or maybe you'd rather talk about roast pork with provolone and broccoli rabe, the actual sandwich of Philadelphia, a line I've parroted so many times, it's also starting to feel like its own cliché? Is anything original anymore? In the all-encompassing vortex of social media, you've gotta wonder. When I was interning at *Philadelphia* magazine in 2005 for April White, who was the food editor at the time, I received a bulleted paper printout of the book's cardinal sins. Never use the word "unique," it commanded (I still don't), and avoid clichés.

In that spirit, I've tried to avoid clichés in this 2019 update of *Philadelphia Chef's Table*. I've added 15 restaurants (and culled many more that have closed or tumbled off the cliff of relevance), and some of them are obvious choices: How can we do this without talking about Vernick Food & Drink in Rittenhouse Square or South Philly Barbacoa in the Italian Market, each massively influential in its own right? But we'll also dive into a yellow curry from Hardena, the beloved Indonesian lunchroom in Newbold, and crackling Filipino-style lechon from Lalo, a shiny new stall in the revitalized Bourse food hall in Old City, because their stories haven't been told often enough. We'll shoot over the bridge to Zeppoli, the Sicilian stronghold, for pasta and down I-95 to Terrain's enchanted Garden Cafe, where wildly creative desserts hide among the potted plum trees and wisteria vines, because "Philadelphia" doesn't just mean the city proper. We'll explore Chinese-Hawaiian long rice that contains no actual rice and Afro-Caribbean jerk chicken masquerading as fried chicken, because these dishes, much like the town in which they're served, are not always what people expect.

"There's one thing, though, that hasn't changed from our cheesesteak days, when the rivalries between our colorful cheesesteak vendors earned the humble sandwich its place atop Philly foodie lore," White wrote in the previous edition's introduction. "It's still the personalities—the talented chefs, innovative bartenders, and personable owners— that are the driving force behind the city's current restaurant renaissance." We may be in a different stage of evolution than the one she wrote about just seven years ago, but that guiding principle endures.

—*Adam Erace*

STARTERS & SNACKS

We'll start here: Call them "starters," "snacks," or the outdated "appetizers," Philly diners love small plates. We'll order one or two at the bar before dinner—snacks like Friday Saturday Sunday's Oysters with Frozen Meyer Lemon Mignonette (page 3) and Barbuzzo's Bruschetta with Stracciatella & Fava Beans (page 10)—and another one to share at the start of our meal (maybe Vernick's Uni with Scrambled Egg, page 31). At some restaurants, like Nick Elmi's cool little bar In the Valley (page 27), you can make a full, fun meal of a collection of dishes that are small in size and big in flavor.

That's why Philly chefs love small plates, too. This is their opportunity to talk diners into something different and experiment themselves. The best of the city's starters and snacks impress with powerful, surprising flavors, a memorable addition to a restaurant meal or your dinner party.

1

FriDay SaturDay SunDay

Rittenhouse Square
261 South 21st Street
(215) 546-4232
fridaysaturdaysunday.com

"Named after the days it's open, this pretty little restaurant serves a complete dinner for about $6 a person," wrote restaurant critic Jim Quinn in the 1973 issue of Philadelphia magazine. "That's about as much as you'd expect to spend . . . in Chinatown or South Philadelphia, for less food and a lot less atmosphere." Quinn's review of Friday Saturday Sunday, which name-checks dishes like flounder mousseline and Chili Elizabeth Taylor, goes on to be rather kind to the upstart BYOB south of Rittenhouse Square, a restaurant that endured in various iterations until 2015.

Chad and Hanna Williams had never eaten there. Most under-40 Philadelphians who make it their business to eat around had never eaten there. Friday Saturday Sunday had the history in the bricks and stories in the walls, but it hadn't been a relevant restaurant for many years. The Williamses, industry veterans from Jose Garces' restaurants, changed that when they took over the space and reopened in 2016... with the same name. "We always felt we wanted to keep the name because it meant something to the neighborhood and we wanted a restaurant that was for the neighborhood," Chad says.

The couple over-delivered. Sure, Friday Saturday Sunday draws Rittenhouse and Fitler Square residents all week long—they're lucky to have the handsome, marble-topped bar, where Paul MacDonald crafts some of the best cocktails in the city, as their local watering hole. But given Chad's confident, seasoned cooking and the polished service directed by Hanna, the restaurant has become something much greater: a full-fledged destination.

OYSTERS WITH FROZEN MEYER LEMON MIGNONETTE

"I love water ice," says Friday Saturday Sunday chef-owner Chad Williams. "As a kid, I went with my mom to Overbrook Water Ice all the time. Lemon was my favorite, and it occurred to me one day to see if it was a good pairing" for oysters. It is. Williams matches a water ice-esque frozen Meyer lemon mignonette with Price Edward Island as part of the baller seafood plateaus that grace the tables. If you can't find PEI oyster specifically, any crisp, clean East Coast oyster will work.

(SERVES 2-4)

1 cup Meyer lemon juice

½ cup orange juice

½ cup lemon juice

1-2 tablespoons granulated sugar, divided

2 small shallots, sliced ¼-inch thick

1 dozen oysters, shucked in their shells

Combine the citrus juices and 1 tablespoon sugar and whisk until the sugar has dissolved. Taste the citrus mixture; it should be tart with just enough sweetness to cut the acid. Whisk in the remaining sugar as needed.

Add the sliced shallots to the citrus mixture and let them sit for 20 minutes at room temperature. Strain out the mixture into a shallow pan and discard the shallots. Place the pan in the freezer. Once the mixture is frozen, scrape with a fork for create an icy, granita-like texture. Reserve frozen until plating.

Arrange the shucked oysters over ice. Top each with a small spoonful of the frozen mignonette and serve immediately.

© GETTY IMAGES

K'FAR

Rittenhouse Square
110 South 19th Street
(267) 800 7200
kfarcafe.com

Michael Solomonov's first kitchen job was in a bakery in K'Far Saba, his hometown located northeast of Tel Aviv between the West Bank and the Mediterranean. "In Israel, bakeries are really community hubs," says Solomonov, who owns Zahav (page 89), Dizengoff, Abe Fisher, and several other restaurants with partner Steve Cook. "Historically people start and end their days at bakeries, with a pastry in the morning and dinner at night. That's the experience we want to bring to Philly." That experience is K'Far, an all-day cafe and bakery, as well as a showcase for Zahav pastry chef and James Beard Rising Star award-winner Camille Cogswell.

© STEVE LEGATO

"Mike and Steve really had a vision for K'Far," says Cogswell. To help her understand that vision, the partners took Cogswell on a field trip to Israel. "The trip was super influential and inspirational. There were several dishes, like borekas and rugelach, that we knew we were going to have on K'Far's menu, but tasting them in Israel really cemented their significance."

Joining the borekas (recipe follows) and rugelach are pistachio morning buns, tehina chocolate-chip cookies, caper-buttered smoked salmon bagel sandwiches, and a new look for

© ALEXANDER HAWKINS

avocado toast, which Cogswell smacks with the herby green hot sauce schug. As the sun goes down in Rittenhouse, K'Far's menu builds up to heartier entrees like t'bit, an Iraqi-style chicken-and-rice dish typically eaten on the Sabbath, eggplants stuffed with beef braised in Turkish coffee, and even a take on Zahav's legendary lamb shoulder--here's it's a shank braised in sour cherry juice and decorated with pickled rose petals. No reservation required.

KALE & FETA BOREKAS

K'Far owner Michael Solomonov and pastry chef Camille Cogswell have worked on these flaky triangular pastries since 2015. "The borekas are so nurturing and special and familiar to Mike, so developing them has been an intricate process that's been several years in the making," says Cogswell. "We started with his grandmother's original recipe, and together we tested it and tweaked it, mostly for fun; there was no specific end goal." They started popping up on special event and catering menus, and by the time Solomonov and partner Steve Cook announced K'Far, it was a foregone conclusion the borekas would be a fixture of the bakery.

(MAKES 24 SMALL OR 6 LARGE PASTRIES; SERVES 6)

For the filling:

2 tablespoons olive oil

1 medium yellow onion, minced

3 garlic cloves, thinly sliced

Kosher salt

3 cups baby kale, finely chopped

⅓ cup crumbled feta cheese

1 egg

For the borekas:

2 cups all-purpose flour, plus more for rolling

1 tablespoon extra-virgin olive oil

1 teaspoon apple cider vinegar

1 tablespoon kosher salt

1 scant cup seltzer, plus more as needed

8 tablespoons unsalted butter, softened

1 egg, beaten

Poppy seeds, for dusting

Nigella seeds, for topping

White sesame seeds, for topping

To make the filling: Heat the olive oil in a medium saucepan over medium-high heat. Add the onion, garlic, and a pinch of salt and cook for 8–10 minutes, or until the onion is soft and translucent. Add the kale and cook, tossing, until just wilted. Transfer the mixture to a bowl and let it cool. Sprinkle the feta over the kale mixture and stir to combine. Adjust salt to taste. Crack the egg into a mixing bowl, add the kale-feta mixture, and mix well. Reserve cold until borekas are ready to fill.

To make the dough: Combine the flour, oil, vinegar, and salt in a food processor, then add the seltzer. Process until the mixture looks crumbly, then continue for a few minutes more, adding a drop or two more of seltzer until the dough comes together in a ball. Process for 10 seconds, then flour a large cutting board and scrape all the dough onto it. (You can also make the dough by hand in a large bowl with a wooden spoon.)

Press the dough into a rectangle about 6 inches long. (The dough is easiest to work with the closer you get to a perfect rectangle.) Flour your rolling pin and roll the dough out to the size of your cutting board, starting in the center and rolling in a fluid motion, moving your arms and applying gentle pressure instead of pressing down. When you're about halfway there, roll up the dough on the rolling pin, set aside, and flour the board again. Unroll the dough on the board.

Place the butter on one end of the dough and, using a silicone or offset spatula, spread it evenly in long motions over half the dough, leaving a ½-inch border on the edges.

Fold the unbuttered half of the dough over the

buttered half. Fold the edges up and in to keep the butter inside. Fold the right and left edges into the center of the dough and fold in half again to make a book fold.

Sprinkle a bit of flour on the board, then pat the dough down into a perfect rectangle; it should feel smooth. Transfer the dough to the freezer (right on the cutting board, uncovered) for 15 minutes.

Remove the board from the freezer and gently press a finger into the dough; it should feel pliable. If you feel a shard of butter, it has hardened too much, so leave the dough out for a few minutes. You want the dough and the butter to be closer to the same temperature so the butter doesn't crack and they roll out smoothly together.

Working quickly and with just enough flour to keep the dough from sticking to the board and rolling pin, roll the dough out to the size of the cutting board. If the dough sticks to the board, roll it up on the rolling pin, dust the board with more flour, and flip the dough. Sprinkle a little flour on any holes and continue rolling.

Fold the short ends in to meet in the center, then fold the whole thing in half again to create another book fold. Scrape off and discard any extra butter or flour from the board. Pat the dough into a perfect, even rectangle; it should still feel cold.

Return the dough to the freezer for 15 minutes. Repeat this process of making a book fold three more times, freezing it for 15 minutes between each new fold. You will roll out the dough five times total.

Add only as much flour as needed to prevent the dough from sticking to the board and rolling pin.

After the last roll-out and freezing, remove the dough from the freezer. Dust it with flour on both sides, then roll it out one last time to fit the dimensions of the board. Cut the dough into roughly 3-inch squares (about 24) for small borekas or 6-inch squares (about 6) for large borekas. Place the squares on parchment paper-lined baking sheets, cover, and return to the freezer for another 15 minutes, or up to 5 days.

Preheat the oven to 400°F. Remove the dough from the freezer. If frozen for longer than 15 minutes, let it thaw for 10 minutes, or until the squares are pliable.

For small borekas, spoon a little of the filling into the center of each square, brush the edges lightly with egg wash, and fold the dough over to make triangles or rectangles. For large borekas, drop a spoonful or two of the filling just inside one corner of each square, brush the edges lightly with the egg wash, and fold the dough over to make triangles. Gently press the edges to adhere. Brush the tops with egg wash and sprinkle with your choice of poppy, nigella, and/or sesame seeds. Refrigerate on the baking sheet for 15 minutes.

Transfer the borekas to the oven. Bake small borekas for about 25 minutes, larger ones for about 30 minutes, rotating the baking sheet halfway through, until the dough puffs slightly and the tops are golden brown. Serve warm or at room temperature.

BarBUZZO

Washington Square West
110 South 13th Street
(215) 546-9300
barbuzzo.com

When Barbuzzo, the hotly anticipated third restaurant from 13th Street entrepreneurs Marcie Turney (pictured right) and Valerie Safran, opened in 2010, it began collecting accolades as quickly as reservations. In just the first nine months, Frommer's called the Mediterranean restaurant one of the continent's best new urban restaurants. The James Beard Foundation named it a Best New Restaurant semifinalist. And the *New York Times* took notice, praising the holy trinity of toppings on the *uovo* pizza (brussels sprouts, runny egg, and truffle oil) and the caramel budino, a dessert so popular the restaurant began selling it to go.

Turney and Safran hadn't planned on opening another restaurant. The pair was renovating the space to lease it. "Once we stripped the space, it was beautiful," Turney says. "We had to put a restaurant there."

Barbuzzo is a return to Turney's Mediterranean roots and the first of the couple's restaurants to have a liquor license. That means

© NEAL SANTOS

luscious Italian whipped ricotta, Spanish grilled octopus, Portuguese roasted sardines, and basil lemonade cocktails, inspired by trips through Italy.

"I always knew I wanted to do Mediterranean again. That's the food I really love to cook," Turney says. "And everybody loves Mediterranean."

WHIPPED RICOTTA WITH GRILLED FRENCH TABLE BREAD

"This whipped ricotta is by far the easiest recipe ever," says Barbuzzo chef-owner Marcie Turney. "You just put ricotta in a food processor. I didn't know what would happen the first time we tried it, but the texture is amazing, so smooth. We add garnishes depending on the season."

(SERVES 4)

1 cup sheep's-milk ricotta (cow's-milk ricotta can be substituted)

2 tablespoons whole milk

⅛ teaspoon kosher salt

Pinch of black pepper

⅛ teaspoon sea salt

1 tablespoon plus 2 teaspoons extra-virgin olive oil, divided

½ tablespoon vin cotto

⅛ teaspoon fresh thyme leaves

⅛ teaspoon dried oregano leaves

2 figs, cut into quarters

8 slices ½-inch-thick French table bread (Barbuzzo uses Metropolitan Bakery)

⅛ teaspoon kosher salt

⅛ teaspoon black pepper

In a food processor, puree the ricotta, milk, and kosher salt until silky smooth, approximately 30 seconds. Spoon onto a serving plate and press a well into the ricotta with the back of a spoon.

Sprinkle pepper and sea salt over ricotta. Drizzle with 1 tablespoon olive oil and vin cotto. Garnish with thyme, oregano, and figs.

To prepare the bread, brush each side with remaining 2 teaspoons olive oil. Sprinkle both sides with salt and pepper. Grill or toast until browned, 30–60 seconds on each side.

BRUSCHETTA WITH STRACCIATELLA & FAVA BEANS

"This is part of our vegetable board when fava beans are in season," says Barbuzzo chef-owner Marcie Turney. "It's easy and it looks great and it tastes great. When fava beans aren't in season, we make a different type of bruschetta or flatbread."

(SERVES 4)

2 cups fava beans, removed from pods

⅛ teaspoon kosher salt

Pinch of black pepper

⅛ teaspoon lemon zest

½ teaspoon lemon juice

3 tablespoon extra-virgin olive oil, divided

1 tablespoon mint leaves, chiffonade

8 ½-inch-thick slices French baguette

1 clove garlic

Additional kosher salt and black pepper, as needed

¾ cup buffalo mozzarella, torn into strings ("*stracciatella*")

1 tablespoon aged balsamic vinegar

Over high heat, bring a large saucepan of salted water to a boil. Blanch fava beans for 2 minutes. Remove beans and plunge into ice water to stop cooking. Peel and discard tough exterior skin. This should yield 1 cup peeled fava beans. In a small bowl, mash fava beans with a fork. Add ⅛ teaspoon kosher salt, pinch of black pepper, lemon zest and juice, 1 tablespoon olive oil, and mint and fold ingredients together.

Brush baguette slices with 1 tablespoon olive oil and rub cut sides with garlic clove. Season with salt and pepper. Grill or toast until lightly crisped, 15 seconds on each side.

Top each baguette slice with mozzarella and mashed fava beans. Garnish with remaining 1 tablespoon olive oil and balsamic vinegar.

THE INGREDIENTS: METROPOLITAN BAKERY

When Metropolitan Bakery opened its doors in Rittenhouse Square nearly twenty years ago, the shop's artisan European breads were an oddity. "Our first customers thought our breads were burnt!" says owner Wendy Born of the richly caramelized, wild yeast boules and slender baguettes that line the bakery.

Now, those loaves—in country white, whole wheat, organic spelt, and a dozen other combinations—are a city institution and a restaurant go-to. You'll find Metropolitan rolls in restaurants' bread baskets and in their recipes. Chef Marcie Turney uses Metropolitan breads for Barbuzzo's Whipped Ricotta with Grilled French Table Bread (page 10), a simple combination that relies on top-notch ingredients.

As the demand for those "burnt" breads steadily increased, Born and Metropolitan's meticulous baker, James Barrett, expanded the business, opening several more storefronts—always with coffee and a little sample of customer favorites—and an around-the-clock baking facility in Port Richmond, where the loaves are still shaped by hand. The Metropolitan brand has grown, too, to include small sweets (like the delicious, hard-to-find canele) and cakes, addictive, award-winning granola, and, most recently, a sophisticated take on popcorn, in flavors like stout-almond, bourbon, and spiced peanut butter. Visit metropolitanbakery.com

RITTENHOUSE SQUARE

sampan

Washington Square West
124 South 13th Street
(215) 732-3501
sampanphilly.com

"Chefs have so much more fun cooking appetizers than cooking entrees," admits chef Michael Schulson (pictured right). "Entrees are a commitment. Appetizers are an experiment," he says, offering one explanation for the city's enduring fleet small-plates restaurants. Sampan, his stylish-but-affordable modern Asian spot, was one of the firsts.

Once the chef-owner of Izakaya in Atlantic City, Schulson was a largely unknown quantity when he opened Sampan in 2009, back when Midtown Village was in the early days of its transition to dining juggernaut. . Now, with his wife and business partner, Nina Tinari, he's become one of the city's most prolific restaurateurs, with a portfolio that includes Harp & Crown, Double Knot, Alpen Rose, Giuseppe & Sons (with the Termini family), and Osteria (with Jeff Michaud).

© SCHULSON COLLECTIVE

Despite Sampan's status as Schulson's resident senior the place still packs them in. Among the small-plate experiments that have earned Sampan and Schulson notice: crab wonton tacos, a Sriracha-spiked Philly cheesesteak on a Chinese bun, his famous edamame dumplings (first created by Schulson for Buddakan, page 69), everything on the popular dim sum brunch menu and, quite unexpectedly, miniature cones of soft-serve ice cream in flavors like Fruity Pebbles and Snickers. This is a restaurant that likes to surprise. The sleek dining room—sip a mango-cardamom sour and watch the cooks in the open kitchen carefully plate ceviche—doesn't hint at the casual Graffiti Bar tucked into a colorful courtyard behind the restaurant, where scorpion bowls with crazy straws are the drink of choice.

"As a chef, I always want to do something fun for my diners," Schulson says.

SWEET SHRIMP WITH RADISH & CITRUS SALAD

"This dish is flavorful yet subtle, combining succulent shrimp with a sweet citrus aioli and earthy radish for texture and balance. Topped with fresh lime segments and baby cilantro leaves, it's bright and fresh but also satisfying," says Sampan chef-owner Michael Schulson. "I love it with a glass of crisp white wine in the summer or a hearty wheat beer in the winter. Take care not to overcook the shrimp, in order to preserve their meaty texture."

(SERVES 4–6)

For the shrimp:

1 cup mayonnaise

1 lemon, juiced

1 lime, juiced

½ cup sweetened condensed milk

1 teaspoon kosher salt

2 teaspoons granulated sugar

¼ cup grape seed oil

½ cup pineapple juice

4 cups vegetable oil

24 U-15 shrimp, peeled and deveined

2 cups cornstarch

Additional kosher salt, as needed

Special equipment: Thermometer

For the salad:

1 lime, juiced

1 lemon, juiced

1 orange, juiced

½ cup grape seed oil

1 teaspoon honey

Kosher salt and white pepper, as needed

2 limes, segmented, membrane removed

2 stalks celery, thinly sliced

3 radishes, sliced into matchsticks

1 red chile, minced

To prepare the shrimp: Begin by whisking together mayonnaise, lemon juice, and lime juice in a bowl. Whisk in condensed milk, salt, and sugar. While whisking, slowly add grape seed oil and mix well. Continue whisking and slowly add pineapple juice and mix well. Set sauce aside. (Sauce can be made up to 4 days in advance and stored, covered, in the refrigerator.)

In a large heavy-bottomed pot, heat vegetable oil to 350°F. Toss shrimp in cornstarch, shaking off any excess coating. Fry shrimp in batches until golden brown and crispy, 3–4 minutes. Remove shrimp from oil with tongs or a metal strainer. Drain on paper towels. Season with salt. Toss shrimp with sauce to coat well.

To prepare the salad: Begin assembling the salad by combining lime, lemon, and orange juices with oil and honey in a bowl. Season with salt and white pepper. Toss lime segments, celery, radishes, and chile with dressing.

To serve: Divide the salad between plates. Top each salad with the shrimp.

BEEF LETTUCE CUPS WITH TOMATO SALAD

"When I cook Asian food, I don't want to do what Chinatown does. I think, 'What is a Michael Schulson take on this?'" Sampan chef-owner Michael Schulson says. "I ask, 'What do people think of when they think of a lettuce cup?' Then I deconstruct it. It doesn't look like the lettuce cup you would expect."

(SERVES 4)

¼ cup sake or dry white wine

½ cup soy sauce

½ cup grape seed oil

12 ounces skirt or flank steak

½ red onion, finely diced

1 tomato, diced

½ Thai red or jalapeño chile, sliced thin

1 clove garlic, chopped

3 basil leaves, chiffonade

¼ cup cilantro leaves, chiffonade

½ cup bean sprouts, chopped

4 tablespoons red wine vinegar

¼ cup extra-virgin olive oil

Kosher salt and white pepper, as needed

1 head Bibb or iceberg lettuce, leaves cut in 2-inch circles

½ cup roasted peanuts, chopped

In a large bowl, combine sake or white wine, soy sauce, and grape seed oil. Marinate steak in mixture, refrigerated, for 1 hour.

Light grill or preheat broiler. Remove steak from marinade. (Discard marinade.) Grill or broil steak for 7 minutes on each side (medium rare) to 12 minutes per side (well done). Allow meat to rest for 5 minutes. Slice beef into 1-inch cubes, slicing across the grain.

In a bowl, combine onion, tomato, chile, garlic, basil, cilantro, and bean sprouts. Toss with vinegar and olive oil. Season with salt and white pepper.

Place lettuce rounds on a serving plate. Top each with salad and a piece of meat. Garnish with peanuts.

DISTRITO

University City
3945 Chestnut Street
(215) 222-1657
distritorestaurant.com

When chef Jose Garces and his staff traveled to Mexico City to sample the capital's distinctive street food, they booked hotel rooms in Zona Rosa, the city's raucous nightlife district. The garish energy of Zona Rosa—and the flavors they discovered at the hectic, vibrant Mercado de la Merced—was the inspiration for Distrito, Garces's third restaurant.

"Bienvenidos!" announces green neon, welcoming diners to the bubblegum pink dining rooms plastered with movie-style marquees advertising south-of-the-border beers and signature margaritas. Over here, Mexican movies, projected on a big screen. Over there, a wall of six hundred *lucha libre* masks. There, diners crowded around a table in a vintage green and white VW Beetle, a nod to Mexico City's ubiquitous taxis. (And behind that door, a purple private karaoke room.)

Garces was also the opening chef at restaurateur Stephen Starr's El Vez. Distrito shares that restaurant's over-the-top Mexican pop culture–inspired decor, but Garces has refined his approach to Mexican flavors. At El Vez, the seven signature guacamoles—"Bazooka Limon" with goat cheese, "Caesar Chavez" with pasilla-balsamic sauce—are prepared tableside on a tricked-out bicycle. At Distrito, a far more traditional guac is served in a sleek silver sphere, with lush crab. Ceviche is topped with lime sorbet, tongue gets the taco treatment, and duck, rabbit, and pork belly star in the mole.

"Mexican food has been a part of my fabric since I grew up in Chicago surrounded by Mexican restaurants," says Garces. "Distrito gives me the freedom to do Mexican food my way."

VERACRUZ CEVICHE

"You wouldn't see a Veracruz ceviche in Mexican cuisine," says Distrito chef-owner Jose Garces. "We took what is traditionally a stew-y sauce made for red snapper, a very hearty sauce, and turned it into a delicate, chilled sauce with some spice and the brininess of capers and olives for ceviche. It works."

(SERVES 4)

For the Veracruz sauce (makes 1¼ cups):

¼ Spanish onion, diced

2 garlic cloves, crushed

2 tablespoons extra-virgin olive oil, divided

Kosher salt, as needed

2 beefsteak tomatoes, seeded and diced

1 cup clam juice

½ cup tomato juice

1 bay leaf

1 teaspoon Mexican oregano

2 sprigs thyme

1 tablespoon cinnamon

1 clove

1 teaspoon black peppercorns

Special equipment: Cheesecloth

For the fish:

½ pound red snapper loin

¾ cup prepared Veracruz sauce, divided

4 teaspoons minced green olives

¼ cup diced Roma tomato

4 teaspoons small-diced red onion

1 tablespoon chopped cilantro

1 tablespoon chopped flat-leaf parsley

½ cup extra-virgin olive oil

¼ cup lime juice

Kosher salt, as needed

For serving:

4 teaspoons capers

24 avocado "pearls"

24 sprigs micro oregano

Special equipment: Small melon baller

To prepare the Veracruz sauce: Combine onion, garlic, and 1 tablespoon olive oil in a medium saucepan over medium heat. Season with salt. Sweat until softened but not browned. Add tomato, season with salt, and cook about 15 minutes. Add clam juice and tomato juice and bring to a simmer. Make a sachet of cheesecloth filled with bay leaf, oregano, thyme, cinnamon, clove, and peppercorns. Add to pan and cook for 30 minutes. Remove sachet and discard. Transfer sauce to a blender and puree until very smooth. While the blender is running, add remaining 1 tablespoon olive oil in a slow stream, blending until emulsified. Season with salt. Chill.

To prepare the fish: Using a very sharp knife, slice red snapper into thin slices. Spread 1 tablespoon Veracruz sauce on each of the four plates. Fan fish over the sauce. In a bowl, combine olives, tomato, red onion, cilantro, parsley, olive oil, lime juice, and remaining ½ cup Veracruz sauce. Mix well and season with salt. Spread mixture over fish.

To serve: Garnish dish with capers, avocado pearls created using the melon baller, and micro oregano. Serve immediately.

PHILADELPHIA ICON: PHILLY PRETZELS

Let's set this straight first: The coveted term "Philly pretzel" can't be applied to just any twist consumed within city limits.

We love the big, butter-brushed, pastry-like Pennsylvania Dutch soft pretzels, but those are not the Philly pretzel. And we love hard snack pretzels, consuming twice the national average of crunchy twists, nuggets, rods, matchsticks, and crisps. But none of those are the Philly pretzel either.

As any Philadelphian knows, the true Philly pretzel is a very particular thing: a salt-dotted, double-looped, smooshed oval of a pretzel, crisp on the top and the bottom and chewy on the sides, where it has been torn from a tray of identical twists. The proper Philly pretzel is served with mustard and waxed paper—or a brown box, when you buy by the dozens to share with coworkers or classmates. The best are still warm. We eat them for breakfast—and just about any other time.

It might be fair to say that since the region's German ancestors introduced the Old World creation in the 1700s, there's been only one universally acceptable variation on the original: spontaneous "P"-shaped pretzels when the Phillies win the World Series.

© NICK TROPIANO/SHUTTERSTOCK.COM

Bistrot La Minette

Queen Village
623 South 6th Street
(215) 925-8000
bistrotlaminette.com

"This is what an authentic bistro looks like," says Philadelphia-born, French-trained chef Peter Woolsey, surveying his first restaurant. Authenticity was Woolsey's mantra when he opened Bistrot La Minette. Yellow walls are painted with wood stain to mimic years of cigarette smoke that the restaurant will never see. Black-and-white images of the French countryside hang above lipstick red banquettes. A carafe of easy-drinking house wine sits on almost every marble table.

This is what a bistro tastes like: *bouchées à la reine aux champignons sauvages* (wild mushrooms in puff pastry), *lapin rôti à la moutarde* (mustard-braised rabbit), and *mille feuille aux framboises* (puff pastry with raspberries). Crisp *gougères,* compliments of the chef, start each meal; house-made chocolates arrive with the check.

And Woolsey's French-born wife, Peggy Baud—who lent her name and recipe for the popular *gratin de pâte* "à la Peggy" (mac and cheese)—teaches the Philadelphia-accented waitstaff the proper pronunciation of these home-style French dishes, so that the bustling restaurant even *sounds* French.

But the sign by the door says it best: *Ici, les vins sont fins et la cuisine soignée.* "Here, the wines are fine and the kitchen cared for."

OEUF DU PÊCHEUR

"A long time ago, I took a trip up through Normandy, and I had this dish in a little seafood restaurant in Honfleur," says Bistrot La Minette chef-owner Peter Woolsey. "I forgot about it until I came across it in a book. Now it's a staple in the restaurant. It's decadent, without having many of the ingredients that you think of as decadent."

(SERVES 4)

50 Blue Bay or Prince Edward Island mussels

3 tablespoons unsalted butter, divided

2 cloves garlic, roughly chopped

1 large shallot, sliced

1 cup white wine

2 cups heavy cream

4 slices thick-cut country-style French bread

1 cup white wine vinegar

4 cups water

4 large eggs

¼ cup chopped tarragon

1 large egg yolk

Kosher salt and white pepper, as needed

Special equipment: Thermometer

To prepare the mussels: Scrub with a brush to remove any seaweed or grit.

In a large saucepan with a lid, melt 2 tablespoons butter over medium heat. Sweat garlic and shallots in butter until softened but not browned. Add mussels and white wine and cover. Cook mussels until they open, about 5 minutes.

Strain mussels, garlic, and shallots from the broth, reserving mussels and broth. Return broth to saucepan and bring to a boil over high heat. Reduce broth by half. Add cream and reduce broth by half again. Reduce to a simmer. Remove mussels from shells, reserving mussels and 12 shells, for presentation.

Toast bread and spread with remaining 1 tablespoon butter. Keep hot in a warm oven.

In a small saucepan, combine white wine vinegar and water to 180°F to poach eggs. (See "Step by Step," page 46.) Poach until just set, about 4 minutes. Using a slotted spoon, remove eggs from water and place on buttered toast.

Add tarragon to broth. Whisk in egg yolk and continue to simmer to thicken. (Do not boil as broth will curdle.) Season with salt and white pepper. Add reserved mussels. Once heated through, divide between four plates, spooning mussels and broth over each egg and garnishing with mussel shells.

Alma De Cuba

Rittenhouse Square
1623 Walnut Street
(215) 988-1799
almadecubarestaurant.com

The idea for a Latin restaurant had been on Stephen Starr's mind for a long time. Latin, in fact, had been the original concept for the space that became Buddakan (page 69).

"I was going to Miami a lot in the late '80s and early '90s," Starr says. "I was in love with all the little Cuban places, classic places like Versailles, and modern places like Yuca."

Versailles is as close to Cuba as most can legally go, a four-decade-old Little Havana landmark known for its homey pre-Castro cooking. Yuca—an acronym for Young Urban Cuban-Americans—is the next generation of that Cuban cuisine. Yuca, which opened in 1989, and its superstar chef, Douglas Rodriguez, invented the term "Nuevo Latino cuisine."

Starr partnered with Rodriguez to create Alma de Cuba, bringing his sexy style of Cuban food and cocktails like the passion fruit Alma Colada—and not incidentally, Rodriguez protégé Jose Garces, who would go on to open Amada (page 93) and numerous other Philadelphia hot spots—to Walnut Street.

The dimly lit restaurant, illuminated by portraits and landscapes from its namesake island, dresses up the classic flavors of Cuba—chorizo is sandwiched in a slider with classic Cubano additions pickle and mustard; fried oysters top fufu, the traditional mashed plantain dish; and recognizable sour orange mojo sauce shares the menu with a unique maple version. For dessert: chocolate-dusted almond cake "cigars," with a gold-foil Alma de Cuba cigar band and a book of sugar matches.

EMPANADA DE VERDE WITH ONION CONFIT & ARTICHOKE ESCABECHE

"We wanted to make something vegetarian that would be exciting and appeal to everyone," says Alma de Cuba chef Douglas Rodriguez. "Usually, when you see a vegetarian dish, it consists of the same usual suspects of ingredients, like mushrooms since they're meaty. We wanted to do something different, and this dish actually incorporates vegetables in both the crust and filling."

(SERVES 4)

For the onion confit:

1 yellow onion, diced

1 sprig rosemary, leaves only

1 teaspoon red pepper flakes

2 cloves garlic

½ cup extra-virgin olive oil

Kosher salt and black pepper, as needed

For the artichoke escabeche:

2 tablespoons olive oil

4 artichokes, trimmed and hearts sliced very thinly

¼ cup apple cider vinegar

2 tablespoons honey

1 tablespoon flat-leaf parsley, chopped

1 piquillo pepper, julienned

1 lemon, juiced and zested

For the empanadas:

2 green plantains, peeled and cut into 1-inch
    pieces

2 teaspoons kosher salt

¼ pound yucca, diced small

2 cups whole milk

Additional kosher salt and black pepper, as needed

2½ pounds baby spinach

2 tablespoons olive oil

2 cloves garlic, chopped

1 yellow onion, diced small

8 ounces manchego cheese, grated

8 cups canola oil

Special equipment: Food mill or ricer,
    thermometer

To prepare the onion confit: In a small saucepan
over medium heat, combine all ingredients for the
onion confit mixture and season with salt and pepper. Simmer until everything has softened, about 30
minutes. Place mixture in a blender and blend until
smooth. Refrigerate until ready to use.

To prepare the artichoke escabeche: Heat olive oil
in a sauté pan over medium heat. Sauté artichokes
until soft, 3–4 minutes. Add vinegar and honey to
deglaze the pan, cooking until almost dry. Remove
pan from heat and add parsley, pepper, and lemon
juice and zest. Refrigerate until ready to use.

To prepare the empanadas: Place plantains in a
medium saucepan. Add water to cover and season
with 2 teaspoons salt. Boil over high heat until plantains are very soft, about 1 hour. Remove plantains
and process with a food mill or ricer. Allow dough to
cool slightly and shape into 8 balls. Place each ball
between two sheets of plastic wrap and use a rolling
pin to roll dough to about ¼-inch thick. Refrigerate
until ready to use.

© STARR RESTAURANTS

In a medium saucepan over low heat, combine
yucca and milk. Simmer until yucca is tender, about
1 hour. Place mixture in a blender and blend until
smooth. The mixture will thicken like a light cream
sauce. Set aside.

Fill a large saucepan with water, season with salt,
and bring to a boil over high heat. Add spinach and
blanch until wilted, about 1 minute. Remove spinach
and plunge into ice water to stop cooking. Once
cool, remove spinach and squeeze out remaining
water. Place in a mixing bowl.

In a medium sauté pan over medium heat, heat olive
oil and sweat garlic and onion until softened but not

browned. Add onion mixture to mixing bowl with spinach.

Slowly add yucca mixture to spinach-onion mixture, stirring until it resembles creamed spinach. (You may not use all the yucca mixture.) Add cheese and season with salt and pepper. Refrigerate until ready to use.

To make empanadas, divide spinach filling between plantain rounds, mounding filling in the center of the dough. Fold dough in half and crimp the edges with a fork. Refrigerate for 3 hours to set.

In a large, heavy-bottomed pan, heat oil to 350°F.

Place 1 or 2 empanadas at a time into the oil and fry until deep golden brown and crispy. Remove from oil and season with salt.

To serve: Divide escabeche and onion confit between four plates and top with empanadas.

In The Valley

East Passyunk
1615 East Passyunk Avenue
(267) 858-0669
itvphilly.com

Nick Elmi had a problem. Laurel, the intimate BYOB he opened in 2013 on East Passyunk Avenue, was becoming more ambitious and acclaimed every year but was hamstrung by its lack of a liquor license.

"Even though we were a BYOB, we all took wine service very seriously; everyone in our front-of-house is a first- or second-level sommelier," says Elmi, who in 2016 found a solution in the shuttered cafe next door. He took over the space, dropped an interior door between it and Laurel, installed a bar, and secured a liquor license that could be shared between both establishments. He called the new bar In the Valley, the Lenape translation for Passyunk.

Laurel got its wine list, but South Philly got its first legit cocktail bar—not to mention one that's put a spotlight on meticulously made non-alcoholic drinks as Elmi has become serious about sobriety. (A summery, smoked pineapple elixir has such voluptuous smokiness you'd swear there was mezcal in the glass.) And since this is a Nick Elmi joint, smart and interesting food is an integral part of the experience. ("We have a reputation to uphold," he says.) Think of the menu as Laurel Lite: same exacting standards placed on the ingredients, same inventiveness in pairings, same super-tight execution, but stripped down just enough to make sense for In the Valley's setting. Grilled, yuzu kosho'ed prawns the size of popsicles. Fall-off-your-barstool biscuits, made sometimes with duck fat, sometimes with dry-aged beef fat. Rabbit schnitzel spiked with fermented brassicas from the Laurel cellar. "It's still snacky food, just not chicken fingers."

© NEAL SANTOS

SMOKED TROUT MOUSSE ON PUMPERNICKEL TOAST

"I'm a huge, huge fan of smoked fish," says In the Valley's chef-owner Nick Elmi. This trout mousse has been on the menu from day one, piped over butter-seared soldiers of pumpernickel from local baker Mighty Bread.

(SERVES 10)

1 stick unsalted butter

1 loaf of pumpernickel bread, cut into 30 (3)-inch-long bars

1 pound cream cheese, softened

1¼ cups sour cream

1⅓ cups extra-virgin olive oil

6 smoked rainbow trout fillets, about 24 ounces total

1 tablespoon plus 2 teaspoons Worcestershire sauce

1 tablespoon Tabasco sauce

½ teaspoon Diamond Crystal kosher salt

For serving:

1 red radish, thinly sliced

Trout roe

Mixed micro-herbs

Melt the butter in a skillet over medium heat and working in batches, toast the bars of pumpernickel on all sides. Remove the toasts and allow to completely cool.

While the toasts are cooling, make the mousse. Combine the cream cheese, sour cream, olive oil, trout, Worcestershire, Tabasco, and salt in the bowl of a stand mixer fitted with the paddle attachment. Mix on high speed for 1 minute, then lower the speed to medium and continue to mix until all the ingredients are incorporated. Transfer the mousse into a piping bag and pipe down the length of each cooled piece of toast. Garnish with radishes, roe, and micro-herbs. Serve 3 pieces per person.

vernick food & drink

Rittenhouse Square
2031 Walnut Street
(267) 639-6644
vernickphilly.com

Before founding one of the most influential restaurants in town, Greg Vernick was a nomad. He worked for Jean Georges Vongerichten's global restaurant group, bouncing around between JGV outposts (Tokyo, Dubai, Vancouver, Park City), and by 2010, the South Jersey native was ready to come back home. "My parents were here, Julie and I were newly married," he says. "It was time to get ready for a family and the long game."

The Vernicks found a bi-level townhouse just off Rittenhouse Square and renovated it into a spare, sophisticated space with a bar and open kitchen on the first floor and aerie-like dining room upstairs overlooking Walnut Street. When it opened in 2012, Vernick Food & Drink was the best expression of a modern American restaurant at the time, a place in which kumquat-jeweled fromage blanc toast and softly scrambled eggs topped with uni (recipe below) coexisted with an earnest wood-roasted chicken and whole bass wreathed in charred citrus and Shishito peppers. This was Vernick's vision from day one, "a take, on the classic American restaurant," he says. "In the time prior to opening, I'd visit my parents and friends and notice a shift in the energy and landscape in Philly. With each trip home, I'd realize more and more that it was the city I could try out the idea I had been nurturing."

The city responded enthusiastically, lifting Vernick to James Beard nominations (he won Best Chef Mid-Atlantic in 2017) and eventual expansion with Vernick Fish and Vernick Coffee at the new Four Seasons hotel. Meanwhile the original restaurant has maintained its essential character over the years—it very deeply feels like and is regarded as a Philadelphia classic despite its relative youth, and the menu has that rare ability to comfort one moment and thrill the next.

UNI WITH WARM SCRAMBLED EGGS & WHIPPED YOGURT

The uni with warm scrambled eggs was the first dish on Vernick's opening menu that Philadelphia lost its mind over, and it's become too much of a signature to take off the menu. It's a study in soft, luxurious textures that's surprisingly easy to make. Equipment note: iSi whipped cream dispensers can be purchased at most kitchen stores and online.

(SERVES 2)

For the shrimp butter:

1 pound fresh shrimp

2 tablespoons grapeseed oil

1 teaspoon tomato paste

⅛ cup brandy

4 sticks unsalted butter

For the whipped yogurt:

½ cup low-fat or nonfat yogurt

¼ cup heavy cream

Pinch cayenne pepper

⅛ teaspoon lemon juice

Pinch of kosher salt

Special equipment: iSi whipped cream dispenser and NO₂ canister

For the uni and eggs:

1 cup beaten extra-large eggs

Pinch of cayenne pepper

Pinch of Diamond Crystal kosher salt

Pinch of very thinly sliced scallions

⅓ pound fresh East or West Coast
   sea urchin gonads

Sea salt, for serving

Peel the shrimp and measure out 1 cup of shells for this recipe. Reserve the shrimp for a future use. Heat the grapeseed soil in a medium pot over medium-high heat until it begins to smoke. Add the shells and saute until they begin to caramelize and become very aromatic, about 3 minutes. Stir in the tomato paste and lower the heat to medium. Deglaze with the brandy and continue to cook until the liquid has almost completely evaporated. Add the butter and cooked until just beginning to brown, about 10 minutes. Strain off the butter small

mixing bowl and discard the solids. Measure out and reserve 1½ tablespoons of shrimp butter for the continued recipe. The remainder can be stored in an airtight container in the fridge for one week or the freezer for three months.

To make the whipped yogurt: Gently mix all ingredients in a medium mixing bowl and load into the ISI dispenser. Charge with 1 pump NO₂. Shake well and refrigerate until serving.

To make the scrambled eggs: Place the eggs, the reserved 1½ tablespoons of shrimp butter, kosher salt, and cayenne in small pot over low heat. Whisk the egg mixture to create small, soft scrambled curds. The eggs should be runny but not watery, and the texture should be more like custard than traditional scrambled eggs. Remove them from heat just before they appear to be done, as to account for carry-over cooking. Adjust seasoning with cayenne and kosher salt to taste, then fold in the scallions. Divide the eggs between two small serving bowls and top with the uni and the whipped yogurt. Garnish with sea salt and serve immediately.

SOUPS & SALADS

It's a predictable question: "Soup or salad?" The answer, in Philadelphia, is both—with the promise that nothing about the city's best soups and salads is predictable.

Peruse the menu and it's quickly clear that our chefs' inspirations aren't iceberg lettuce and chicken noodle.

Hearts of palm get the classic French stew treatment at Vedge (page 36), bacon and eggs star in the traditional central France Salade Lyonnaise at Parc (page 45), and watermelon is treated as a green as the central component of Kanella Grill's savory feta and almond–topped salad (page 52). Remember: These flavorful dishes don't have to be considered sides. On a warm summer day, Tria's Grilled Asparagus Salad (page 49) and a glass of Chenin Blanc is all you need, and when the mercury dips, Poi Dog's ginger-spiked Hawaiian-Chinese Chicken Long Rice (page 55) will warm you right up.

VEDGE

Washington Square West
1221 Locust Street
(215) 320-7500
vedgerestaurant.com

"This is a vegetable moment," says Vedge chef-owner Rich Landau, surveying the nation's dining scene. Landau was well ahead of the trend. He has been cooking gourmet vegan food in Philadelphia for seventeen years, first at vegan Horizons in Willow Grove, then at the restaurant's reincarnation near South Street, which he closed in 2011. Now there's Vedge, the vegetable-focused destination in Washington Square West widely regarded as the eminent vegan restaurant in the country. "There's a lot of people out there who would come to a 'vegetable restaurant' but wouldn't come to a 'vegan restaurant,'" Landau says.

Housed in the former Deux Cheminees, Vedge is a sexier, more sophisticated version of Horizons, with both small plates—a vegetable bar will plate "vegetable charcuterie," like Landau's portobello carpaccio—and larger vegetable-centric entrees.

The inspiration for Vedge was Los Angeles's "meat-meat-meat" Animal. "We really want to be that vegetable counterpart," Landau told the Philly food media when the restaurant opened, "which is ironic, because they're in L.A. and we're here in Philly, and it really should be the other way around."

A seitan chef in a cheesesteak town, Landau is constantly challenged to convince diners that vegetables are as satisfying a meal as meat. He's his own toughest audience. "I became a vegetarian when I was a teenager for ethical reasons," he says. "But I was already a carnivore. My palate already knew those flavors. I turn vegetables and proteins like tofu into great meals so that I don't crave meat." It's working; Landau is a multiple-year James Beard Award nominee for Best Chef Mid-Atlantic, and Vedge has spawned two offshoots, casual V Street in Rittenhouse Square, and Fancy Radish in Washington, D.C.

CHILLED CUCUMBER-AVOCADO SOUP WITH SMOKED PUMPKIN SEEDS

"This soup is inspired by one I ate in Nicaragua," said Vedge chef-owner Rich Landau. "The minute I tasted it, I said, 'This is on the menu the minute we get back.' The key to the soup is the texture of the cucumber. It's like shaved ice. That's the food processor. If you made this with a blender, it would be a watery mess."

(SERVES 4)

For the soup:

4 cucumbers, peeled, seeded, and chopped

¼ cup loosely packed mint leaves

¼ cup loosely packed cilantro leaves

1 ripe avocado, roughly chopped

¼ cup white onion, chopped

¼ teaspoon ground cumin

¼ teaspoon curry powder

2 tablespoons extra-virgin olive oil

¼ cup vegan mayonnaise or sour cream

2 teaspoons Dijon mustard

Juice of 2 limes plus more as needed

1½ teaspoons sea salt plus more as needed

1½ teaspoons black pepper

½ teaspoon agave syrup or granulated sugar

1 cup water

For the pumpkin seeds:

½ pound shelled, raw pumpkin seeds

2 teaspoons smoked paprika

1 teaspoon ground cumin

1 teaspoon sea salt

2 teaspoons olive oil

For serving:

Additional extra-virgin olive oil, as needed

To prepare the soup: Puree all ingredients in a food processor to a smooth, creamy consistency. Chill for 1 hour. Taste and adjust lime or salt as needed.

To prepare the pumpkin seeds: Preheat oven to 400°F. Toss pumpkin seeds with spices and oil and bake until seeds brown and become fragrant, 7–10 minutes. Set aside.

© GETTY IMAGES

To serve: Pour soup into four bowls and garnish with pumpkin seeds and olive oil.

HEARTS OF PALM, BEACH STYLE

"This funky recipe is my take on a beachside soup that you might find in France or the French Caribbean, using hearts of palm instead of fish," says Vedge chef-owner Rich Landau. "It's a pretty cool recipe: easy, with amazing results."

(SERVES 4)

4 tablespoons olive oil, divided

1 cup leeks, chopped

1 clove garlic, minced

¼ cup white wine

8 cups vegetable stock

2 cups Yukon Gold potatoes, diced

1 tablespoon Old Bay or other seafood seasoning

1 teaspoon fennel seeds

Sea salt and black pepper, as needed

2 cups plum tomatoes, diced

2 16-ounce cans hearts of palm, drained, rinsed, and cut into 1-inch pieces (2 12-ounce packages of fresh hearts of palm can be substituted)

½ teaspoon saffron threads

1 tablespoon tarragon leaves, chopped

1 baguette, cut into 1-inch slices and toasted

In a saucepan over medium-high heat, heat 2 tablespoons olive oil. Add leeks and garlic and sauté until fragrant, 3–5 minutes.

Add wine. Reduce heat and simmer until reduced by half.

Add vegetable stock, potatoes, seafood seasoning, and fennel seeds. Season lightly with salt and pepper, and simmer until potatoes are almost cooked, about 8 minutes. Add tomatoes, hearts of palm, and saffron. Cover and simmer until potatoes are fully cooked, 5–10 minutes.

Stir in tarragon and remaining 2 tablespoons olive oil. Season with salt and pepper again. Divide between four bowls and serve with toasted baguette slices.

OYSTER HOUSE

Rittenhouse Square
1516 Sansom Street
(215) 567-7683
oysterhousephilly.com

The Oyster House feels of-the-moment—light and airy, lined with bright subway tiles—until you get a tour of the restaurant from owner Sam Mink. The milk-glass cocktail rail at the front of the restaurant was salvaged from Kelly's, a classic Philadelphia fish house that Mink's grandfather Samuel bought in 1947. The oyster plates hanging on the wall are part of the Mink family's two-hundred-plus plate collection, gathered through a half century of shucking. Server Lorraine Steele has been with the family for more than three decades, and that quirky Philadelphia favorite fried oyster and chicken salad has been on the menu just as long.

Mink's father, David, opened the original Sansom Street Oyster House in this spot in 1976 and ran it until his retirement in 2000. The business was sold and then shuttered. In 2009, Sam reopened the restaurant, in the same Sansom Street location, minus the Sansom Street name, reigniting the city's dying fish house tradition.

"There were no traditional fish houses left in Philadelphia," says the third-generation restaurateur. "I want to re-create the Oyster House for Philadelphia, with hints of the past while moving toward the future." So there's the snapper soup, a fish house standard too often known elsewhere for its thick cornstarch texture. At the Oyster House, the soup starts with whole snapping turtles, served with top-notch sherry from the bar.

"Old school, new school—we use those terms a lot," Mink says. "Oyster House bridges the gap."

OYSTER STEW

"The traditional oyster stew is just oysters and cream, but we wanted something a little fresh and exciting for the new Oyster House," says Oyster House owner Sam Mink. "Anise flavors and oysters pair very well together so we add fennel to the stew and garnish it with tarragon. 'Shrubbery,' that's what some of the old-timers call the new stuff we've put in there. They request it 'without shrubbery,' just classic oysters and cream, which we are happy to do, too."

(SERVES 4)

1 tablespoon unsalted butter

2 cups leeks, sliced

2 cups fennel, sliced

6 cups heavy cream

1 tablespoon Worcestershire sauce

2 dashes Tabasco or other hot sauce

Kosher salt and black pepper, as needed

24 oysters, shucked

1 lemon, zested

2 tablespoons tarragon, roughly chopped

In a large saucepan over medium heat, melt butter. Cook leeks and fennel until tender but not browned. Add heavy cream and cook over medium heat until the mixture has reduced enough to coat the back of a spoon, about 20 minutes. Add Worcestershire sauce and hot sauce. Season with salt and pepper.

Reduce heat to bring cream mixture to a simmer. Add oysters and their liquid. Poach gently until oysters plump in the middle and shrivel around the edges, 1–2 minutes. Add lemon zest and tarragon. Divide between four bowls and serve immediately.

NEW ENGLAND CLAM CHOWDER

"Gulf Coast and West Coast oysters are fine, but we are an East Coast oyster bar," says Oyster House owner Sam Mink. "Our New England clam chowder is a staple dish for our East Coast–centric seafood menu. It's the perfect combination of briny clams, sweet cream, and creamy potatoes." **Note:** Chowder is best when made a day in advance.

(SERVES 4)

© TIM TAI

12 cherrystone clams

4 cups clam juice

1 cup bacon, diced

2 cups Spanish onion, diced

2 cups celery, diced

2 tablespoons unsalted butter

6 tablespoons all-purpose flour

2 sprigs thyme

1 bay leaf

2 cups russet potatoes, diced

2 cups heavy cream

Kosher salt and black pepper, as needed

In a medium saucepan with a tight fitting lid, combine clams and clam juice. Cover and bring to a boil over high heat. Reduce heat to low and simmer until clams open, 10–15 minutes. Strain, reserving clams and clam stock. When cool, remove clams from shells and finely chop clams. Set aside.

In a separate medium saucepan over medium heat, cook bacon until fat renders and bacon crisps. Add onion and celery and sweat until softened but not browned, about 5 minutes.

Add butter. When butter melts, add flour and cook for 1 minute. Add thyme and bay leaf. Slowly add reserved clam stock, stirring, to avoid clumps. Lower heat and bring to a simmer, skimming any impurities that rise to the surface with a ladle.

Add potatoes and heavy cream and continue to simmer until potatoes are tender, 10–15 minutes. Remove herbs and season with salt and pepper. Add chopped clams.

ROUGE

Rittenhouse Square
205 South 18th Street
(215) 732-6622
rouge98.com

Oh, Rouge. There are so many stories to be told about Rouge (. . . engagements, weddings, affairs, divorces, celebrities canoodling in the corner . . .), each more outrageous than the next (. . . and then founder Neil Stein was imprisoned for tax evasion . . .). So much so that the only thing that can surprise people is that all of this—plus a ¾-pound burger that *GQ* ranked as one of "The 20 Hamburgers You Must Eat Before You Die"—happened in a dining room that's just eight hundred square feet.

Since its opening in 1998, Rouge has loomed far bigger in the psyche—and on the sidewalks—of Rittenhouse Square, spilling out onto 18th Street with coveted bistro tables that doubled the restaurant's seating capacity and launched the city's outdoor dining scene. The French-influenced restaurant transformed a former state liquor store into a never-ending cocktail party, hosted by the restaurant's regulars. To be a regular takes commitment—the most recognized faces have been frequenting the restaurant nearly daily for more than a dozen years—but the reward is a sidewalk seat facing the square on the first sunny spring day.

"Rouge has become a piece of the fabric of Philadelphia," says Rob Wasserman, who now owns the restaurant with his wife, Maggie (who also happens to be Neil Stein's daughter). "It's timeless."

BIBB & ENDIVE SALAD

"I created this dish in 1999, when a lot of people were doing a Bibb and endive salad. I wanted to do it a little differently, with spicy cashews," says former Rouge chef Michael Yeamans. "The dish has stood the test of time. It is still one of our top sellers."

(SERVES 4)

For the spiced cashews (makes 3¼ cups):

3¼ cups unsalted cashews

1 tablespoon ground cumin

1 tablespoon paprika

½ tablespoon ground cayenne pepper

½ tablespoon chile powder

½ tablespoon kosher salt

½ tablespoon black pepper

½ cup granulated sugar

¼ cup hot water

For the red wine vinaigrette (makes 4¼ cups):

1 cup red wine vinegar

¼ cup Dijon mustard

2 tablespoons honey

Kosher salt and black pepper, as needed

2 cups vegetable oil

1 cup extra-virgin olive oil

For the salad:

2 endives

2 heads Bibb lettuce, separated into leaves

1 cup grape tomatoes, cut in half

½ cup red onion, julienned

1 cup apple, sliced

2 tablespoons shallot, minced

2 tablespoons flat-leaf parsley, chopped

2 tablespoons chives, chopped

½ cup prepared red wine vinaigrette

For serving:

1 cup crumbled Roquefort cheese

To prepare the spiced cashews: Preheat oven to 300°F. In a large bowl, mix cashews with spices. In a separate bowl, combine sugar and water, mixing until sugar is dissolved. Add sugar water to cashews, stirring until fully combined. Spread cashews on a baking sheet and cook until nuts appear dry, about 15 minutes. Let cool.

To prepare the red wine vinaigrette: Whisk together red wine vinegar, mustard, and honey in a bowl. Season with salt and pepper. In a separate bowl, whisk together vegetable and olive oils. Slowly drizzle oil into vinegar mixture, whisking until emulsified.

To prepare the salad: Cut endives into quarters, lengthwise. Remove core and slice thinly length-wise. Toss endive, lettuce, tomatoes, red onion, apple, shallots, parsley, and chives with red wine vinaigrette.

To serve: Divide salad between four plates. Garnish with cheese and 1 cup prepared spiced cashews.

parc

Rittenhouse Square
227 South 18th Street
(215) 545-2262
parc-restaurant.com

Parc, Stephen Starr's sprawling, spectacular French brasserie on Rittenhouse Square, was almost a deli.

"That's what the owners of the building originally wanted," says Starr, a restaurateur renowned for his endless supply of restaurant concepts. He pauses to consider: "This isn't that much different from a deli, really."

Age-tarnished mirrors, salvaged brass fixtures, French-language newspapers, and the city's best baguette aside, Starr has a point: The bistro is France's answer to the deli, serving up a classic menu, three meals a day, in a casual, convivial environment. Plus—this is key—a bar, the same gleaming zinc beacon you'd find in a Paris classic.

And then there's the inimitable location, stretching down 18th Street along the park—those bistro chairs, all turned to face Rittenhouse Square, a warming sight even on blustery winter days—and turning on to quieter Locust Street, where

© NEAL SANTOS

en plein air diners might hear the city's next protégé practicing at the Curtis Institute of Music.

At 7:30 a.m., the restaurant is a quiet refuge for an omelet and a cafe au lait. At noon, it is business meetings over *moules frites*. At 3 p.m., people watching and onion soup gratinée. At 5 p.m., happy-hour cocktails and oysters. At 8 p.m., lingering over steak frites and roast chicken, crème brûlée and tarte tatin, and a carafe of wine. Weekend brunch—sleep in, the restaurant doesn't even open its doors until 10—is croissants, Champagne, and towers of fruits de mer.

"Breakfast, lunch, or dinner. This is where you bring your friends and celebrate your life," says Starr.

SALADE LYONNAISE

One of the most classic and recognizable dishes in French cooking, this salad is a perfectly calibrated balancing act. The bracing acid of the dressing and the bitterness of the frisée cut the fat of the egg yolk and the bacon.

(SERVES 4)

3½-inch-thick slices brioche, crust removed, cut in 1-inch cubes

½ cup plus 2 tablespoons olive oil, divided

Kosher salt and black pepper, as needed

½ cup sherry vinegar

1½ teaspoons Dijon mustard

½ cup vegetable oil

1 tablespoon white vinegar

4 large eggs

2 tablespoons unsalted butter

½ pound bacon, cut in ½-inch cubes

2 russet potatoes, cut in ½-inch cubes

8 cups torn frisée, dark green leaves discarded

⅓ cup flat-leaf parsley leaves

⅓ cup tarragon leaves

⅓ cup chervil leaves

1 shallot, finely chopped

STEP BY STEP: POACHING AN EGG

1. Heat
In a saucepan, combine 8 cups of water and 1 tablespoon white vinegar. The vinegar will help keep the egg whites from spreading during cooking. Heat to 180°F, which is barely simmering.

2. Crack
Crack eggs into individual bowls. This prevents egg shells from falling into the poaching water and allows you to add the eggs to the water more gently.

3. Swirl
With a spoon, swirl heated water to form a whirlpool. The motion will keep the egg whites close to the egg yolk and prevent the egg from dropping to the bottom of the pan.

4. Cook
Carefully add egg to swirling water. Cook for 4 minutes. Remove from water with a slotted spoon and drain on a paper towel. Gently press egg with one finger to ensure that the whites are set and the yolk remains liquid.

5. Serve
Serve immediately or allow to cool, returning poached eggs to barely simmering water until reheated before serving.

Preheat oven to 350°F. To make croutons, toss bread cubes with 2 tablespoons olive oil and sprinkle with salt and pepper. Spread in a single layer on a baking sheet and bake, turning once, until golden brown, about 10 minutes.

To make the vinaigrette, combine sherry vinegar and mustard. In a separate bowl, combine remaining ½ cup olive oil and vegetable oil. Slowly pour oil mixture into vinegar mixture, whisking vigorously until emulsified.

To poach eggs, bring a large saucepan filled with water to a simmer. Add white vinegar. Gently slide the eggs, one at a time, into the simmering water. (See "Step by Step," page 46.) Cook until whites are just set, about 4 minutes. Lift poached eggs out of water with a slotted spoon and place in a bowl of warm water until serving.

In a sauté pan over medium heat, melt butter until sizzling. Add bacon and cook slowly until crisp on all sides, about 10 minutes. Remove bacon. Add potatoes to bacon fat in sauté pan and cook until golden brown. Remove potatoes, sprinkle with salt, and drain on paper towels.

In a large bowl, combine frisée, parsley, tarragon, chervil, and shallots. Add bacon, potatoes, and croutons and toss together. Drizzle salad with vinaigrette and toss. Divide salad between four plates. Place a poached egg at the center of each plate and serve.

Tria

Two locations: Rittenhouse Square and Washington Square West
18th and Sansom Streets, (215) 972-8742
12th and Spruce Streets, (215) 629-9200
triacafe.com

Even Tria owner Jon Myerow seems surprised by the success of this small wine, beer, and cheese bar. "It's amazing to me that some of our top-selling wines are varietals that people 'don't' drink, like Chenin Blanc and Zweigelt," he says. That was the goal from the start: to introduce Philadelphia, already starting to discover craft beers, to artisanal beers, wines, and cheeses, without any of the pretension that comes with the words "wine bar." (And without the signature cocktails that were a mainstay of the Rittenhouse Square scene; Myerow recalls that when the restaurant opened in 2004, the first customer tried to order a cosmo.)

One popular Chenin Blanc is described on the frequently changing menu in a mixture of traditional wine speak and honest enthusiasm: "Redolent of honeyed pear, fig, and citrus with a mineral rich finish from the man, Bruwer Raats." Cheeses are "ice cream for grown-ups" (a beer-washed cow's-milk cheese from Wisconsin), a "cream-infused pillow" (classic Brillat-Savarin from France), and "eminently lemony and fresh" (a Massachusetts goat's-milk cheese). Beer is categorized from "invigorating" to "extreme." No matter the adjectives, the offerings all have one thing in common. "Everything is made by real people," Myerow says.

The Tria vibe—99 percent enjoyment, 1 percent education—caught on quickly. A second Tria location followed, and the restaurant launched the Tria Fermentation School to offer wine, beer, and cheese classes. A beer-focused spin-off, Tria Taproom, opened in 2013.

"When we opened Tria, there was nothing else like it," says Myerow. "There's still not enough places like it."

GRILLED ASPARAGUS SALAD

"Our menu is hard to define. We call it 'wine bar cuisine' because it is a little Spanish, a little Italian, a little of all of the Mediterranean countries you think of as wine countries," says Tria owner Jon Myerow. "It's all of those things, and this salad is a great example because it has all of those Mediterranean flavors."

(SERVES 4)

2 tablespoons smooth Dijon mustard

¼ cup red wine vinegar

1½ cups canola oil

Kosher salt and black pepper, as needed

1 pint grape tomatoes, sliced into thirds

1 roasted red bell pepper, diced

2 tablespoons red onion, chopped

12 stalks asparagus, trimmed, grilled, cooled, and cut into 1½-inch pieces

1 cup Ruggiero or other Italian-marinated artichokes, sliced

2 cups Divina or other white beans

4 large slices rustic whole wheat bread

2 tablespoons extra-virgin olive oil, divided

3 tablespoons pine nuts, toasted

1 lemon

In a blender or food processor, combine mustard and vinegar. While processing, slowly add oil until emulsified. Season vinaigrette with salt and pepper. Combine vinaigrette with tomatoes, red bell pepper, and onion, mixing well to coat. Allow relish to sit at least 1 hour. (It can be made up to 2 days in advance.)

In a large bowl combine asparagus, artichokes, and white beans. Using a slotted spoon, scoop relish onto salad. Add vinaigrette to taste.

Brush bread with 1 tablespoon olive oil and grill or toast until edges are crisp. Cut each slice into thirds and arrange in the center of each plate. Spoon salad on top of bread. Garnish with remaining 1 tablespoon olive oil, pine nuts, and a squeeze of lemon juice.

TENAYA DARLINGTON: PHILADELPHIA'S MADAME FROMAGE

"My mother is from Switzerland, and I spent my formative years in Wisconsin, so dairy has always been in my blood," says Tenaya Darlington. The local author and writing professor, who got her start penning the popular Madame Fromage blog in the early aughts, has a new feather in her cap: Tria's Director of Cheese. "I had always loved Tria and couldn't turn down the opportunity to select cheeses for the entire city," she says. "We have a lot of talented people producing pasture-based cheeses at creameries within a few hours of the city. The local scene is ripe."

© VIRGINIA PRICE

Tenaya Darlington's Favorite Local Cheeses

Witchgrass, Valley Milkhouse
A velvet pyramid dusted with charcoal, from a tiny start-up creamery in Berks County

Cloud Nine, Yellow Springs Farm
A cream puff of goat's milk with a downy rind, from Chester County

Hummingbird, The Farm at Doe Run
Creamy and bloomy, just like an Italian Robiola but made nearby in Chester County

Ba.1mboozle, Goat Rodeo Farm & Dairy
A sultry beer-washed goat cheese from Pittsburgh that tastes like prosciutto and pears

Tomme de Linden Dale, Linden Dale Farm
French-style table cheese made with raw goat's milk from a 7th generation farm in Lancaster County

Trilby, Cherry Grove Farm
A funk bomb washed in Dad's Hat Rye Whiskey, from Lawrenceville, New Jersey

Smokey Noble, PA Noble Farm
A Lancaster County organic cheddar naturally smoked over hickory chips, subtle and buttery

Birchrun Blue, Birchrun Hills Farm
Pennsylvania Stilton, made by beloved farmstead cheesemaker Sue Miller

KANELLA GRILL

Washington Square West
1001 Spruce Street
(215) 922-1773
kanellarestaurant.com

Kanella opened the doors to its simple, white-washed dining room on April 27, 2008, Greek Easter Sunday—"for a little luck," chef-owner Konstantinos Pitsillides says, and the superstition has paid off for the popular BYOB.

This isn't a Greek restaurant as you might know it. The fiercely authentic chef shudders at the stereotype of Americanized Greek food and draws the distinction even more brightly: "A lot of people think that this is a Greek-Greek restaurant, but it is a Cypriot-Greek restaurant, which means more spice and Middle Eastern influences."

Pitsillides is Cypriot, born in the coastal city of Limassol. His wife is Philadelphian, which explains how the flavors and philosophy of Pitsillides's Mediterranean upbringing arrived at the corner of 10th and Spruce. "This is the simple food I grew up with," Pitsillides says.

The opinionated chef has a lot more to say. He'll rail against new trends that aren't new at all or chefs who spend their time whining instead of cooking, often in missives posted in his kitchen window. The lure of a larger space and liquor license convinced Pitsillides to relocate Kanella to Queen Village in 2015, recasting the original as the more casual Kanella Grill. When the risky relocation ultimately failed, he retreated back to 10th and Spruce, where the food—warm hummus topped with ground lamb, whole fish with seasonal greens, spice-braised goat—is as vibrant and elemental as ever.

WATERMELON SALAD WITH FETA & ALMONDS

"We often create dishes by accident—and by tomorrow I won't remember what I did tonight, so we're changing things everyday," says Kanella chef-owner Konstantinos Pitsillides. "I had a watermelon and in my country we often pair it with *halloumi*. Here I used feta. I like the sweetness of the watermelon, the salty sourness of the anchovies, and the freshness of the greens with the creaminess of the feta."

(SERVES 4)

1 cup water

½ cup granulated sugar

¼ cup rose water (available at Middle Eastern markets)

¼ cup extra-virgin olive oil

½ large, heavy watermelon, flesh cut in medium cubes

1 yellow tomato, chopped

20 white anchovies (available at Italian markets)

½ cup slivered almonds, toasted

⅓ pound Greek feta

½ cup mint leaves

1 cup scallions, finely chopped

Kosher salt, as needed

1 teaspoon black pepper

In a saucepan over medium-high heat, combine water, sugar, and rose water. Cook until sugar dissolves and mixture begins to thickens, about 15 minutes. Chill. Whisk in olive oil to emulsify.

Toss watermelon and tomato with rose water mixture. Arrange watermelon and tomato on a platter and top with anchovies, almonds, crumbled feta, mint, and scallions. Season with salt and pepper.

POI DOG

Rittenhouse Square
100.5 South 21st Street
215-279-7015
poidogphilly.com

The genesis of Poi Dog is in the Classics department at Bryn Mawr College, where classmates Kiki Aranita and Chris Vacca hatched a plan for a food truck in 2013. The name comes from Aranita's Hawaii heritage; five generations of her father's family has called the islands home. "It's a non-derogatory term that means mixed breed or mutt in Hawaiian Pidgin English and is used to describe both dogs and people," says Aranita, who grew up in Hawaii and Hong Kong and is Philly's sharpest scholar on the 50th State's vibrant and varied culinary tapestry. "Hawaii's local food is the result of many immigrant cultures cooking together for generations, using the fruits and produce found in and brought to the islands as well as the tinned rations introduced by the American GIs. Sugarcane and pineapple plantation brought groups of laborers from all over the world and so we have

© NEAL SANTOS

adopted foodways from China, Japan, Korea, the Philippines, Portugal, Puerto Rico and many other cultures and married them with indigenous Polynesian ingredients and methods."

In 2017 Aranita and Vacca took Poi Dog to the next phase, opening a brick-and-mortar restaurant near Rittenhouse Square. They kept the casual, counter-service style of the truck but expanded the menu to include exquisite tuna poke and lomi lomi salmon. Proteins like slowly braised kalua pig and ethereally crisp mochi nori fried chicken anchor lunch plates heaped with macaroni salad and white rice. Desserts include Filipino-style bibinkas and chewy, flower-shaped butter mochi in flavors like pandan and chocolate.

Poi Dog has become something of gathering place for Philly's small but tight Hawaii community. "Even when we were just a truck we drew in people who were homesick," says Aranita. "Now, we have a constant rotation of both people who moved here from Hawaii for work or school, even professional baseball and football players who are here to play and belong to mainland teams and want to introduce their teammates to the food they miss." Though the most important guest you might spot outside Poi Dog is Aranita's black-and-tan Chihuahua, Coconut, whose favorite outfit is a Spam musubi sweater.

CHICKEN LONG RICE WITH SCALLIONS AND CRISPY CHICKEN SKIN

"The Chinese were the first to arrive in Hawaii as plantation laborers, so they've been part of Hawaiian cuisine for a very long time," says Poi Dog chef-owner Kiki Aranita. "Chicken long rice is something you always see at luaus." The dish, which starts with a gingery from-scratch chicken stock, exists somewhere between a soup and noodle bowl. Serve it with chopsticks and a spoon.

(SERVES 4-6)

2 pounds bone-in, skin-on chicken thighs

Kosher salt and black pepper, to taste

2 tablespoons unsalted butter

1 cup shoyu

½ cup chicken stock

¼ cup mirin

4 dried shiitake caps, roughly chopped

⅓ cup yellow onion, roughly chopped

4 garlic cloves, roughly chopped

1 inch ginger, washed and roughly chopped

1 (5.3-ounce) pack bean-thread noodles

3 scallions, thinly sliced for serving

Preheat oven to 300°F. Skin the chicken thighs and scrape excess fat away from the skin. Pat the skins dry and lay them over a sheet of parchment in a baking pan in a single layer, preventing skins from touching. Season the skins with kosher salt to taste and lay another sheet of parchment on top. Press under a second sheet pan and reserve.

Season the skinned chicken thighs with salt and pepper to taste. Melt the butter in a shallow roasting pan over medium-high heat. Brown the thighs in batches, being careful not to crowd the pan, about 2 minutes per side. Return all the chicken to the pan and add the shoyu, stock, mirin, shiitakes, onion, garlic, and ginger. Cover the pan tightly with two layers of aluminum foil and transfer to the oven, along with the prepared pan of chicken skins. Bake for 45 minutes.

While the chicken bakes, soak the bean-thread noodles in warm water for 15 minutes. Strain off the noodles and rinse under cool running water. Add the noodles to a pot and cover with fresh water by at least an inch. Bring the pot to a boil and cook the noodles until soft enough to bite through but still retaining some elasticity, 8-10 minutes. Strain off the noodles and reserve.

When chicken is finished cooking, remove the thighs from the pan. Strain out the braising liquid, discarding the solids and reserving the liquid. Bring half the liquid to a simmer in a medium pot over medium heat. Meanwhile, check the skins; if they're crispy, remove them from the oven and transfer to a plate lined with paper towels. If they're still soft or pliable, bake an additional 10 minutes.

When the chicken thighs are cool enough to handle, shred and reserve the meat, discarding bones, fat, and cartilage. Add the reserved noodles to the simmering braising liquid and cook for 5 minutes. If the noodles fully absorb the liquid, add more of the braising liquid to achieve a slightly soupy consistency. Add the shredded chicken and stir to combine. Divide the soup between 4-6 bowls, top with sliced scallions and crispy chicken skins, and serve immediately.

© CAROLINE HATCHETT

Pastas

Philadelphia is a pasta town. Red gravy is a religion in some segments of South Philly. It's hard to compete with *nonna*, but the city's best (and, perhaps, bravest) chefs have made their mark with pastas that go beyond the Sunday dinner table.

A new pasta culture is taking shape—and it is taking every shape, from common spaghetti, pappardelle, and ravioli to less-familiar *tesaroli* (a crepe-style noodle) and *tortelli* (a half-moon take on ravioli). In their pasta dishes, Philadelphia chefs are exploring all of Italy, drawing inspiration from Rome, Lombardy, and Tuscany, but their culinary travels don't end there.

Talula's Garden adopts potato gnocchi to celebrate the mushroom harvest of nearby Kennett Square (page 71); Buddakan goes around the world to transform the ravioli with edamame (page 69); and Han Dynasty reminds us that Italy doesn't have a hold on the world's great noodles with the Szechuan classic Dan Dan Noodles (page 77).

FORK

Old City
306 Market Street
(215) 625-9425
forkrestaurant.com

Since Ellen Yin opened it in 1997, Fork has been a Philadelphia fixture, one that has remained an anchor of Old City dining through several reinventions. Chef Terence Feury reinvigorated the restaurant during his seafood-focused tenure from 2009 to 2013, after which Eli Kulp relocated to Philly from one of New York's hottest restaurants at the time, Torrisi Italian Specialties, and took over as Fork's head chef, and everything changed. Not only did Kulp instantly elevate Fork's game. He elevated the city's entire dining game, bewitching us with bread pairings, alt-grain pastas, dry-aged duck feasts, and other things Philly hadn't really seen before.

Kulp threw himself into his new home, delving deep into the region's culinary history with "Our Terroir" tastings and forging deep connections with local farmers. He and Yin formed a partnership and opened High Street on Market next door, in the former Fork etc. space, and it instantly became one of the most influential bakeries in town. High Street expanded to University City and New York,

© NEAL SANTOS

and Kulp and Yin also took over A.Kitchen in Rittenhouse Square. Not bad for a young restaurant group.

Fork remains the company lighthouse and is as vital as ever, with its central bar busting all hours and a crowd that includes bespoke suited politicians and T-shirt-clad musicians in equal supply. Yin, a perennial James Beard nominee for the Outstanding Restaurateur award, has kept the space fresh with smart and stylish renovations. And though Kulp's role has changed since he was paralyzed in the May 2015 Amtrak crash, he is still the backbone of the kitchen.

"I meet with the different chefs throughout the week, developing dishes and making sure that we're on target with direction and style, as well as mentoring young cooks to grow and develop into strong chefs and leaders," he says. "We still pride ourselves on great hospitality and delicious food, but we're committed to continuing to stay on the leading edge of the Philadelphia dining scene and progressing the food culture in our great city."

SUCKLING PORK TORTELLINI

Boundary-pushing pastas became an integral part of Fork, and later High Street on Market, under Kulp's direction, but these tortellini are a fairly straightforward homage to Philly's favorite roast pork. You can make the tortellini ahead of time and freeze them for up to a month. Kulp suggests adding seasonal vegetables like fava beans or peas to the finished dish.

(SERVES 4)

For the pork filling:

1-2 pounds boneless pork shoulder

Kosher salt and black pepper, to taste

2 tablespoons extra-virgin olive oil

1 small yellow onion, chopped

2 stalks celery, chopped

2 garlic cloves, lightly crushed, plus 3 tablespoons minced

½ cup dry white wine, such as pinot grigio

1 bay leaf

4-5 cups water

Zest of 4 lemons

2½ cups grated Parmigiano-Reggiano

For the pasta dough:

6 egg yolks

¼ cup water

1 tablespoon extra-virgin olive oil

1¼ cups all-purpose flour, plus more for kneading

½ cup durum flour

For finishing the dish:

2 tablespoons unsalted butter

2 tablespoons water

Salt and black pepper, to taste

Grated Parmigiano-Reggiano, for serving

Lemon zest, for serving

Toasted breadcrumbs, for serving

Preheat the oven to 350°F. Season pork generously with salt and pepper. Add the olive oil to a Dutch oven or large, heavy-bottomed pot and set it over medium-high heat. When the oil is warm, brown the pork on all sides and set aside. Add the onion, celery, and the 2 smashed garlic cloves and sweat until the onions and celery are translucent, about 7 minutes. Add the wine to deglaze, scraping up the brown bites from the bottom of the pot with a wooden spoon. Return pork to the pot, add bay leaf and enough water to just cover. Cover the pot with lid or aluminum foil and transfer to the oven. Allow the pork to braise for 1½-2 hours or until the meat easily shreds with a fork.

When the pork has been braising for about an hour, make the pasta dough. Combine both flours in a large mixing bowl and form a well in the center. Add the yolks, water, and olive oil to a medium mixing bowl. Pour the wet ingredients into the well of the flours and stir gently with a fork or your hands, allowing the flour to gradually incorporate into the wet ingredients. Once a ball has formed, turn the dough out onto a clean and floured surface and begin to knead, adding flour when necessary to prevent sticking. Knead 6-8 minutes until the dough is smooth when stretched, making sure it is not sticky. Wrap dough in plastic and rest in the refrigerator for 30 minutes.

Remove the pot from the oven and allow the pork to cool in the braising liquid. When cool enough to hand, remove and pull the pork, then finely chop it. Add the pork to a large mixing bowl and add the minced garlic, lemon zest, and cheese. Season with salt and pepper to taste and reserve for filling.

Bring large pot of generously salted water to a boil. Divide the rested dough into 4 roughly equal portions. Sheet the pasta dough to the thinnest setting on a countertop pasta roller, starting at the widest setting and working your way down to the thinnest. Cut each pasta sheet into 2-x-2-inch squares. Place about 1 tablespoon of pork filling in the center of a pasta square. Moisten two edges of the square lightly with water using your finger or a pastry brush. Join opposite corners of the square together to form a triangle and gently press the moistened dough together, forming a seal. With the point of the triangle facing up, join the 3 points together, forming a tortellini shape. Repeat for remaining pasta squares.

Set a large saucepan with the butter and water over medium heat. Add the tortellini to the pot of boiling water and cook for 4 minutes. Stir or gently shake the saucepan to emulsify the butter and water. Add the tortellini to the saucepan and gently stir until the sauce glazes the pasta and looks shiny. Adjust seasoning with salt and pepper as needed. Transfer the tortellini to a serving platter and top them with Parmigiano, lemon zest, and toasted breadcrumbs. Serve immediately.

ZEPPOLI

Collingswood
618 West Collings Avenue
(856) 854-2670
zeppolirestaurant.com

Most people expected Joey Baldino to open a restaurant in South Philly, where he grew up and where his family has lived for three generations. Instead, after putting in time cooking in Sicily and at Vetri (page 63), where he was chef de cuisine, he skipped over the bridge to Collingswood, New Jersey, a town with a pretty solid dining reputation in its own right. "I was looking in Philly for many years and couldn't find the right spot," he says. "Then the Collingswood space came along, and I had a warm, gut feeling."

© TREVOR DIXON

That feeling didn't let him down. Baldino named his Sicilian BYOB Zeppoli for his favorite dessert, and it became the best restaurant in South Jersey the minute it opened 2011. Some say, it's the best Italian restaurant in the whole Delaware Valley. Either way Baldino, humble to a fault, demurs at the praise. He'd rather put his head down and just cook the food that's in his blood. His father's side of the family is Sicilian, and the island's favorite ingredients fill out the Zeppoli menu: perfumey lemons and magenta prickly pears, salty bottarga and sweet pink prawns, fruity olives and funky cheeses, sweet-and-sour vegetables and pungent herbs. Eating Baldino's robustly flavored, flawlessly executed food in the simply furnished, often cacophonous dining room is a joy, and the experience has a long list of industry fans that willingly make the trek across the Delaware River. Instagram posts from Zeppoli regularly pop up on the feeds of Pizzeria Beddia's (page 144) Joe Beddia and Hungry Pigeon's (page 127) Scott Schroeder. Union Square Hospitality's Danny Meyer comes for summertime Sicilian barbecues on Monday nights. Mike Solomonov of Zahav (page 89) wrote the foreword to Baldino's cookbook.

Baldino is also the chef-owner of Palizzi Social Club, the century-old Italian-American members-only hangout he took over from his uncle in 2017. Unlike his first restaurant, Palizzi is located in South Philly, around the corner where he grew up, and was named one of *Bon Appétit*'s "Hot 10" new restaurants in the country. Baldino divides his time between Palizzi and Zeppoli, but the BYOB will always be the one that gave him that special feeling, "kinda sorta like falling in love with a woman and knowing she's the one."

GNOCCULI ALL'ARGENTIERA

"Gnocculi is Sicilian dialect for gnocchi, and all'argentiera means anything topped with Cacio-cavallo cheese, a mild Sicilian provolone," explains Zeppoli chef-owner Joey Baldino, who first experienced this pasta while studying outside Palermo. "I put this pasta on my opening menu and it has never come off."

(SERVES 6-8)

3.6 ounces fresh spinach

1 large egg

1 pound whole-milk ricotta

2 ounces grated Parmigiano-Reggiano

Pinch sea salt, plus more for salting water

Pinch black pepper

Pinch nutmeg

3 ounces 00 flour

½ stick unsalted butter

12 sage leaves

Grated Caciocavallo cheese, for serving

Bring 2 pots of water, one lightly salted and the other heavily salted, to a boil over high heat. Blanch the spinach for 30 seconds in the lightly salted water, then transfer to a strainer, pressing out as much water from the spinach as possible. Once completely cool, chop the spinach and squeeze out any remaining water. Add the spinach to a large mixing bowl with all the remaining ingredients except the flour. Fold the ingredients together, sprinkling in a little bit of flour at a time to avoid clumping. Taste the dough and adjust seasoning if necessary.

Lightly dust your hands with flour and roll out the dough into round, roughly 1-inch gnocchi. When all the dough has been rolled, drop the gnocchi into the pot of boiling, heavily salted water. Boil for 3 minutes.

While the gnocchi are cooking, brown the butter over medium heat in a skillet until foamy and fragrant. Add the sage leaves, then the cooked gnocchi, tossing to coat. Divide the gnocchi between 6-8 bowls or dishes, generously garnish with grated Caciocovallo, and serve immediately.

VETRI

Washington Square West
1312 Spruce Street
(215) 732-3478
vetriristorante.com

Marc Vetri, modestly describes his goals when he opened Vetri in 1998: "I just wanted to open a nice, little, inviting restaurant like the ones I had been seeing all over Italy." The location, a Washington Square West row home, gave the restaurant that intimate feel—"I wanted it to feel like you were eating in my living room"—and a culinary destiny to fulfill. Vetri's "living room" was the original home of the city's most famous restaurant, Le Bec-Fin.

Vetri was up to the challenge. The restaurant's miniature kitchen has produced memorable dishes—his spinach gnocchi in brown butter, *foie gras* pastrami, and asparagus flan are classics—and launched a new generation of Philadelphia chefs, from Jeff Michaud (Osteria, page 82) to Michael Solomonov of Zahav (page 89) and Joey Baldino of Zeppoli (page 61). A Saturday night reservation for the chef's elaborate tasting menu was the hardest reservation in town—until Vetri transitioned to a tasting-menu-only concept every night.

"Vetri has never stopped evolving," says Vetri. "I've never had to force anything. I've just basically allowed the diners of Philadelphia to make the decisions."

When Vetri sold his restaurant group to URBN, the parent company of Urban Outfitters, in 2014 he wisely kept the Spruce Street flagship out of the deal. And that's where you find him most days, hanging on the stoop, spot-checking the famous roasted goat, or tinkering with esoteric flour blends in the upstairs atelier. Which is not to say Vetri setting into retirement; a branch of the ristorante opened in Las Vegas in

2018, and he's in the process of converting the historic Fiorella's butcher shop in the Italian Market into a casual pasta counter. "I'm having fun, mentoring young chefs, and doing projects that truly inspire me," Vetri says. "Also fixing my espresso machines."

© VETRI CUCINA

SPAGHETTI WITH GREEN TOMATOES & RAZOR CLAMS

"We did this for one of our tasting menus," says Vetri chef-owner Marc Vetri. "We were just kind of messing around. Razor clams have this awesome sweet flavor, and we wanted to think of something that was going to balance it out. Fleshy green tomatoes have a little extra acid and a little bit of a sour flavor, and it worked perfectly. The green tomatoes cook down to make a natural mignonette for the clams."

(SERVES 4)

4 green tomatoes

¼ cup extra-virgin olive oil

1 shallot, diced

½ clove garlic

Kosher salt, as needed

½ pound spaghetti

5 razor clams

Additional extra-virgin olive oil, as needed

To peel tomatoes cut a shallow *x* on the bottom of the tomatoes. Dip tomatoes in boiling water for 10 seconds and then shock them in an ice water bath. Remove and peel. Dice tomatoes.

In a large saucepan over medium heat, heat olive oil. Add shallot and garlic and cook until softened but not browned. Remove garlic and add tomatoes. Cook tomatoes until soft, stirring constantly to prevent browning, about 10 minutes. Reduce heat to low and keep sauce warm.

Bring a large saucepan of heavily salted water to a boil over high heat. Add spaghetti and cook for 2 minutes less than package instructions.

As pasta cooks, open razor clams by sliding a butter knife along open side of shell. Use knife to remove clam. Rinse clams. Coat clams with olive oil and season with salt. Slice clams into pieces as big as coffee beans.

When pasta is done, drain, reserving 1 cup pasta water. Add pasta and reserved pasta water to sauce. Cook over high heat for 2 minutes. Toss with clams and season with salt.

MORIMOTO

Washington Square West
723 Chestnut Street
(215) 413-9070
morimotorestaurant.com

When Morimoto opened in 2001, this Stephen Starr restaurant wowed with its Tokyo-sleek decor, its toro tartare, flavored with house-made soy sauce and freshly grated wasabi, and its omakase menu. The multicourse meal of small dishes—with most of the fish shipped overnight from Tsukiji, Tokyo's famous fish market and prepared by chef Masaharu Morimoto himself—was one of Philadelphia's must-have dining experiences.

Ponytailed and broad-shouldered, chef Morimoto was a striking presence behind the restaurant's sushi bar, wielding his knives to create sushi in the traditional style he learned in his native Japan, with a little *Iron Chef* flair. "You need a sharp knife and a sharp arm," the former baseball player often says. On both the original Japanese cult hit and the later Food Network remake, Morimoto also showed a sharp sense of flavor and a willingness to experiment with it. In Kitchen Stadium, he was known for adding Chinese, French, Italian, and other global flavors to create *Iron Chef*–winning dishes. A Morimoto favorite: soba noodle carbonara. "I don't believe in rules," Morimoto says.

Nearly two decades late, chef Morimoto has opened many more restaurants around the world—including one in New York with Starr—and is better known for his big gestures than his small ones. His visits to Philadelphia might involve carving a two hundred-pound tuna or hosting a big-ticket private charity dinner. But the Iron Chef's influence is strong, and the restaurant remains one of the city's top sushi spots.

 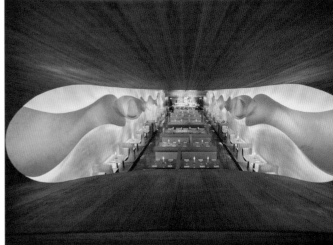

PHOTOS © STARR RESTAUR.

SOBA CARBONARA

"I always say, 'My father is Japanese, but my mother is Italian,'" says Morimoto chef Masaharu Morimoto. "Of course, it's a joke, but I have a lot of recipes in which Italian essence is used, so I have to explain why I use Italian ingredients or techniques to the curious audience. I don't see any boundaries in cooking, so I just thought carbonara sauce should go with soba noodles, too."

(SERVES 4)

½ pound dry soba noodles

1 tablespoon olive oil

3 slices bacon, chopped

½ cup boiled edamame, shelled

24 bay scallops

2 tablespoons white wine

¼ cup water

1 tablespoon soy sauce

1¼ cups heavy cream

3 large egg yolks, beaten

Dash of truffle oil

Kosher salt and white pepper, as needed

Parmesan cheese, as needed

Special equipment: Thermometer

In a large saucepan of boiling salted water, cook soba noodles for 1 minute less than the package directions. Drain well. Toss with olive oil and set aside.

In a large sauté pan over medium heat, cook bacon until fat renders. Remove bacon and drain on paper towels. In the same sauté pan over medium heat, cook edamame and scallops until heated, 2–3 minutes. Add bacon. Turn off heat.

In a saucepan over medium heat, cook white wine to evaporate alcohol. Add water, soy sauce, and cream, and heat to 155°F. Add egg yolks and truffle oil. Season with salt and white pepper. Turn the heat to low and whisk until smooth, being careful not to let the egg yolks cook through. Add reserved bacon, edamame, and scallops and stir. Add soba and stir quickly.

Divide between four pasta bowls and sprinkle with cheese.

BUDDAKAN

Old City
325 Chestnut Street
(215) 574-9440
buddakan.com

Buddakan just might deserve credit for starting it all.

It wasn't Stephen Starr's first restaurant nor was it his first success—both of those distinctions go to the Continental, his Rat Pack martini lounge that relaunched Old City in 1995—but Buddakan's opening in 1998 marked a change in how Philadelphia thought about dining. As quickly as lines formed under the watchful gaze of an eleven-foot gold Buddha, restaurants were exciting and sexy again. No longer were Philadelphians content with just a meal. Buddakan taught diners and the countless future restaurateurs who worked there that dinner was an experience, be it a Hollywood-style Stephen Starr production or an indie BYOB.

It changed how Starr thought about dining, too: "I wasn't really a restaurateur yet, then," says the former concert promoter. "I didn't take it seriously that this was the beginning of a restaurant career for me." Since Buddakan opened its doors, Starr has opened more than twenty other restaurants in Philadelphia—from funky Mexican El Rey (page 85) to classic English pub The Dandelion (page 109) to local-focused Talula's Garden (page 71)—and expanded to other East Coast cities, including opening reincarnations of scene-changing Buddakan in Atlantic City's The Pier Shops at Caesars and New York's Meatpacking District.

EDAMAME RAVIOLI

"I consider the edamame ravioli to be the signature dish at Buddakan," says Buddakan owner Stephen Starr. "It is unique to us and what we do. When we opened Buddakan New York, we created lighter Edamame Dumplings for that restaurant."

(SERVES 4)

For the ravioli:

5 tablespoons unsalted butter, divided

6 shallots, thinly sliced

1⅔ cups chicken stock

Kosher salt and white pepper, as needed

1 pound shelled edamame beans

¼ cup heavy cream

2 tablespoons white truffle oil

32 round wonton wrappers

For the Sauternes-shallot broth:

1½ teaspoons butter

½ cup thinly sliced shallots

½ cup Sauternes wine

1⅔ cups edamame-chicken broth (reserved from preparing ravioli)

2 sprigs thyme

Kosher salt and white pepper, as needed

To prepare the ravioli: In a medium saucepan

over medium high heat, melt 3 tablespoons butter and cook shallots until caramelized. Add chicken stock and season with salt and white pepper. Add edamame beans to broth. Increase heat and bring mixture to a boil. Reduce heat and simmer until beans are tender, 10–15 minutes.

In a small saucepan over medium heat, combine cream and remaining 2 tablespoons butter. Drain beans, reserving beans and broth. (Broth will be used to make Sauternes-shallot broth.) In a food processor, puree beans, working in batches if necessary. Add cream mixture and continue to puree. Transfer beans to a bowl and add truffle oil, mixing well.

Lay out 16 wonton wrappers. Divide filling between wrappers, placing filling in the center of wonton wrapper. Brush edge of each wonton with water

and place another wonton wrapper on top, pressing edges together to seal ravioli.

Fill a large saucepan with water. Bring to a boil over high heat. Cook ravioli for 2½ minutes.

To prepare the Sauternes-shallot broth: In a medium saucepan over medium-high heat, melt butter. Cook shallots in butter until caramelized. Add wine and reduce mixture by one-third. Add broth and thyme and simmer for 30 minutes. Remove thyme and season with salt and pepper. Set aside.

To serve: Divide ravioli between four plates and top with Sauternes-shallot broth.

Talula's Garden

Washington Square
210 West Washington Square
(215) 592-7787
talulasgarden.com

It started with Django, the petite South Street spot that became the benchmark for the Philadelphia BYOB—and the first to receive *Philadelphia Inquirer* food critic Craig LaBan's top four-bell rating. Next Aimee Olexy (pictured below) and her then-husband, Bryan Sikora, sold Django and moved their talents to Kennett Square, where they opened Talula's Table, a cozy cafe and gourmet food shop by day and the nation's toughest reservation after dark. The single farmhouse table—seating twelve—is booked a year in advance. Finally, Olexy returned to Philadelphia to open Talula's Garden with restaurateur Stephen Starr.

Talula's Garden brings a little of Chester County to the city, its dining room extending into the garden courtyard overlooking Washington Square, and the garden extending back into the dining room with tomatoes and herbs flourishing under growing lights. It conjures the fondly remembered Django, with Olexy playing the gracious hostess and a smart, seasonal menu.

And, of course, there is the cheese. Olexy's cheese plate, which she annotated fervently for each table, was a must-order at Django. At Talula's Table, there are the cheese cases, filled with more than one hundred of Olexy's gooey, sharp, stinky favorites. And at Talula's Garden there is, as Olexy calls it, "my land of cheese," a salvaged granite counter with a dedicated cheesemonger that is the centerpiece of the restaurant.

PHOTOS © STARR RESTAURANTS

POTATO GNOCCHI WITH MUSHROOMS & EGG

"This turns your idea of a gnocchi dish upside down," says Talula's Garden owner Aimee Olexy. "It is very light for a gnocchi dish, and you can really taste the potatoes. All the flavors go really well together—and egg is such a great, natural way to enrich the dish—but you can still taste the individual ingredients."

(SERVES 6)

For the potato gnocchi:

4 Yukon Gold potatoes

2 large egg yolks

2 tablespoons plus 1 teaspoon 00 flour (available at gourmet stores)

Pinch of kosher salt

Special equipment: Food mill

For the mushroom jus (makes about 5 cups):

5 black peppercorns

4 carrots, chopped

1 white onion, chopped

1 pound mushrooms

½ cup Madeira wine

4 cups vegetable stock

For serving:

1 tablespoon olive oil

2 pounds exotic mushrooms

¾ cup unsalted butter, divided

1 teaspoon fresh thyme leaves, chopped

2 teaspoons chives, divided, chopped

1 teaspoon lemon juice

½ cup raisins

1 tablespoon ice wine vinegar

6 large egg yolks

18 sorrel leaves

Raw mushroom, shaved (optional)

To prepare the potato gnocchi: Preheat oven to 400°F. Bake potatoes until tender, 45–60 minutes. Scoop out flesh and discard skin. Pass flesh through a food mill. While warm, stir in yolks, flour, and salt. Fold mixture twice, being careful not to overwork. Divide into 4 piles. Roll each into a long tube about 1 inch in diameter. Cut tubes into 1-inch sections to form gnocchi. Roll each gnocchi on the back of a fork to form ridges. Place on flour-dusted surface and allow to rest 10 minutes.

Bring a large pot of salted water to a simmer. Add gnocchi and cook until gnocchi float, about 10 seconds. Store, refrigerated, on a greased pan.

To prepare the mushroom jus: Combine all ingredients in a saucepan over low heat. Simmer for 45 minutes. Strain jus.

To serve: In a sauté pan over medium heat, heat olive oil. Sauté mushrooms until golden, 3–4 minutes. Add 6 tablespoons butter. When melted, add thyme and 1 teaspoon chives.

In a separate sauté pan over medium heat, heat remaining 6 tablespoons butter. Sauté prepared gnocchi until golden, about 2 minutes. Finish with remaining 1 teaspoon chives and lemon juice.

Soak raisins in ice wine vinegar until plump. Puree until smooth.

Divide mushrooms and gnocchi between six plates. Garnish each with raisin puree, egg yolk, sorrel leaves. Divide ¾ cup prepared mushroom jus between plates. Top each plate with shaved mushrooms, if using.

Melograno

Rittenhouse Square
2012 Sansom Street
(215) 875-8116
melogranorestaurant.com

There is a formula for the Philadelphia BYOB: The wife runs the front of the house. The husband runs the kitchen. The hungry diners clog the sidewalk, clutching brown-bagged bottles of wine, waiting for a seat in the tiny no-reservations dining room.

When Melograno opened in 2003, it was just one of dozens of new BYOBs to employ this well-tested formula. Friendly and diplomatic Rosemarie Tran worked the hostess stand. Her Roman-born husband, Gianluca Demontis, cooked in the open kitchen. Would-be diners eyed the restaurant's thirty-four seats and its plates of handmade pastas hopefully.

It was those memorable pastas—pappardelle with truffled mushrooms and walnuts, roasted beet and mascarpone ravioli, traditional carbonara updated with a punch of anchovies—that first set Melograno apart in a town awash in Italian restaurants, BYOBs, and, especially, Italian BYOBs.

"I had worked in a lot of Italian restaurants," Demontis says. "But I wanted to bring the customers my food. Just rustic Italian dishes a little modernized."

With its success, Melograno changed the rules of the BYOB, moving to a space twice as large—but just as loud—as the intimate original and instituting a reservations policy, but you'll still find Tran greeting diners and Demontis tossing pastas.

CARBONARA AL PROFUMO DI TARTUFO BIANCO E ACCIUGHE

"One of my favorite foods is eggs, and the combination of eggs and fish has always worked for me," says Melograno chef-owner Gianluca Demontis. "At home I often make a frittata of anchovies, onions, and eggs. I thought it would make a great combination for carbonara, too. Carbonara has that salty element, so anchovies replace the pancetta in this recipe."

(SERVES 4)

8 salted anchovy fillets

3 large eggs plus 3 large egg yolks, lightly whisked

2 tablespoons white truffle paste or 1 tablespoon white truffle oil

4 tablespoons grated Parmesan cheese

1 tablespoon pistachios, cut in half

2 tablespoons extra-virgin olive oil

2 cloves garlic

14 ounces spaghetti

Sea salt and black pepper, as needed

4 fresh anchovy fillets

Rinse salted anchovy fillets and remove central bone. In a large bowl, mash salted anchovies with a fork. Add eggs and truffle paste or truffle oil and mix gently. Add cheese and pistachios.

In a large sauté pan over medium heat, heat olive oil. Add garlic and cook until browned. Discard garlic. Remove pan from heat.

74 The Philadelphia Chef's Table

In a large saucepan over high heat, bring salted water to a boil. Cook spaghetti to al dente according to package instructions. Drain pasta and add to hot oil. Add egg mixture and cook over low heat, mixing constantly, for 1 minute. Season with salt and pepper. Divide between four plates and top each with a fresh anchovy fillet.

TESTAROLI AL PESTO DI ASPARAGI

"The *testaroli* is an ancient recipe that I found in a history book about medieval life and costume in the Tuscan and Ligurian region when I was in Italy," says Melograno chef-owner Gianluca Demontis. "I like this type of pasta because it really absorb sauces."

(SERVES 4)

2 pounds asparagus

4 cups 00 flour (available at gourmet stores)

4 cups warm water

1 teaspoon sea salt

1 cup almonds, toasted

3 cloves garlic

1 cup olive oil

3 cups basil leaves

1 cup plus 2 tablespoons grated Parmesan cheese, divided

½ cup plus 2 tablespoons grated Pecorino Romano cheese, divided

Additional sea salt and black pepper, as needed

Vegetable oil, as needed

Extra-virgin olive oil, as needed

Over high heat, bring a large saucepan of water to a boil. Blanch asparagus for 2–3 minutes. Remove asparagus and plunge into ice water to stop cooking.

In a bowl, combine flour and water gradually until the consistency of thin pancake batter. Add salt and strain into another bowl. Rest crepe (testaroli) batter for 30 minutes.

In a food processor, combine blanched asparagus, almonds, garlic, and olive oil. Process until well combined. Rest 1 minute, add basil, 1 cup Parmesan, and ½ cup Pecorino Romano, and process until combined to form pesto. Season with salt and pepper.

Lightly coat a crepe pan or sauté pan with vegetable oil. Heat pan over medium heat. Ladle 6 tablespoons of batter into the hot pan, moving ladle in a circular motion over the batter to create a thin, round disc. When the center of the crepe starts to brown, about 30 seconds, flip crepe and cook an additional 15 seconds. Transfer crepe to clean kitchen towel. Repeat with remaining batter to make about 16 crepes.

Cut crepes into bite-size pieces. In a saucepan over medium heat, combine crepe and pesto. Add hot water if pesto is too thick. Cook until warmed. Divide between four plates and top with remaining 2 tablespoons Parmesan, 2 tablespoons Pecorino Romano, and extra-virgin olive oil.

Han Dynasty

Old City
108 Chestnut Street
(215) 922-1888
handynasty.net

Han Chiang is known among Philadelphia diners for two things: his menu of fiery Szechuan dishes and his insistence that you order what he tells you, with the occasional expletive attached to the command. It's all part of the show that has made Chiang's mini-empire of Dynasties a foodie phenomenon.

"Yes, I tell my customer what to eat," says Chiang. "They will place an order, and I will change it for them. They don't know."

There, Chiang has a point. Most Philadelphia diners don't know the traditional Szechuan dishes Chiang takes pride in—three-cup chicken, lion's head meatballs, green bean noodle. They know, to quote the chef, "their crappy Chinese takeout."

"I would rather eat old hot dogs at a 7-Eleven than Americanized Chinese food," Taiwanese-born Chiang says, loudly.

Chiang is known for giving wayward diners just one choice—"Do you like spicy or not spicy?"—but with Chiang's Szechuan menu it's really just a question of spicy or spicier.

At his original suburban location, Chiang grudgingly admits, he serves General Tso's and beef and broccoli alongside the chili oil–spiked classics he evangelizes for. In Old City, Chiang makes no such compromises, and the twenty-course Szechuan banquet he hosts the first Monday night of each month is the hottest ticket in town. "There's so much good Chinese food out there," Chiang says, "but nobody has the guts to do it here. We need to let Americans know what Chinese food is really about."

DAN DAN NOODLES

"The long pole that you carry across your shoulder with a basket on either side—that is called *dan*. Dan Dan Noodles were sold from the baskets with sauce and you mixed it yourself," says Han Dynasty chef-owner Han Chiang. "At the restaurant, I make my own soy sauce and my own chili oil, but even if you don't, this dish is full of flavor. People get addicted to it."

(SERVES 4)

2½ tablespoons vegetable oil, divided

2 ounces ground pork

½ tablespoon minced garlic

2 tablespoons preserved Chinese vegetables (available at Asian markets)

⅓ cup plus ½ tablespoon soy sauce, divided

2 tablespoons sesame paste

2 tablespoons water

2 tablespoons chili oil

½ tablespoon Szechuan peppercorn oil (available at Asian markets)

2½ tablespoons granulated sugar

1 pound flour noodles

Special equipment: Wok

In a wok over high heat, heat ½ tablespoon vegetable oil. Brown the pork and garlic. Add preserved vegetables and ½ tablespoon soy sauce. Remove from heat.

In a bowl, whisk together remaining 2 table-spoons vegetable oil and sesame paste until emulsified. Add remaining ⅓ cup soy sauce, water, chili oil, peppercorn oil, and sugar and whisk until emulsified.

Cook flour noodles according to package instructions.

Pour sauce into an empty serving bowl, add cooked noodles, and top with ground pork. Toss tableside.

ENTREES

Whatever you are craving, you'll find it in Philadelphia. There's Italian and French, of course, but also Mexican and Israeli, Southern and Spanish, Indonesian and English, Filipino and Japanese. And then there's the beloved Philadelphia gastropub, a culinary update on the city's corner bars, where some of Philly's most talented chefs have turned their attention to the roast chicken and burger basics.

These restaurants—and the recipes here—have one important thing in common: They are personal projects, an expression of a chef's culinary identity. Whether a dish had its start in a well-worn family cookbook or was a classic preparation, it has been shaped into something new by the chef's experiences, the region's ingredients, and the Philadelphia diners' expectations.

When cooking at home, the charge is the same. Start with your favorite restaurant's recipe, absorb the cooking wisdom of the city's top chefs—and then cook a dish to meet your own tastes.

OSTERIA

North Philly
640 North Broad Street
(215) 763-0920
osteriaphilly.com

Philadelphia waited nine years. For those nine years, Marc Vetri stayed in the kitchen of his namesake Spruce Street restaurant (page 63), cooking the city's most lauded meals for the lucky few who scored a reservation in the intimate dining room and turning down all offers to open a second spot. (Meanwhile, in those nine years, restaurateur Stephen Starr opened seventeen spots.)

Then, finally, there was Osteria.

That Vetri's sequel opened in a former factory building on a quiet stretch of North Broad Street was a surprise. That Vetri—along with business partner Jeff Benjamin and protégé and partner Jeffrey Michaud—quickly made this North Philly address a dining destination was not. It quickly gained a reputation for crackly-thin pizzas jeweled with peak-season produce, gutsy pastas like the famous chicken liver rigatoni, and flawlessly executed classics like pork Milanese inspired by his Italian mother-in-law.

The partners sold Osteria as part of package deal to URBN, the Philly-based parent company of Urban Outfitters, in 2016, but two years later, Michaud (in partnership with Michael Schulson),

© OSTERIA

bought it back. "It feels great, like having my baby back," says Michaud, a James Beard award-winner. "When I moved back to Philadelphia in 2006 it was to open Osteria. There is a lot of blood, sweat, and tears that went into that place, and I'm very happy to be running it again." These days, Osteria is going through something of a renaissance under the "new" ownership (a new outdoor patio, a hopping happy hour), with the stunningly restored Metropolitan Opera House across the street driving business before and after shows. "Osteria has been going strong for 12 years, and I see it continuing to go strong for many more."

PORK MILANESE WITH ARUGULA SALAD

"My Italian mother-in-law makes this dish the classic way with veal. My wife makes it with chicken. We have a great pig farmer, so I tried it with pork," says Osteria chef-owner Jeff Michaud. "Other than that, this recipe is exactly the way I've had it in Milan. It's a classic that doesn't need to be changed."

(SERVES 4)

4 6-ounce bone-in pork chops

Kosher salt and black pepper, as needed

6 large eggs

2 cups bread crumbs

Unsalted butter, as needed

1¼ cups olive oil, plus additional olive oil as needed

¼ cup lemon juice

3 cups arugula

1 lemon, sliced

½ cup shaved Parmesan cheese

Kosher salt and black pepper, as needed

Pound the pork chops with a meat mallet until about ½-inch thick. Season meat on both sides with salt and pepper. In a bowl large enough to fit a pork chop, whisk eggs. Place bread crumbs in another large bowl. Coat pork chops with egg, then bread crumbs.

In a sauté pan over medium heat, combine equal parts butter and olive oil. When butter is melted, there should be ⅛ inch of the butter-oil mixture. Cook pork chops until golden brown, 3–4 minutes on each side. Drain on paper towels. Season again with salt and pepper.

To assemble the salad, whisk together 1¼ cups olive oil and lemon juice. Toss with arugula. Season with salt and pepper

Divide pork chops between four plates. Top with arugula salad and garnish with lemon slices and cheese.

EL REY

Rittenhouse Square
2013 Chestnut Street
(215) 563-3330
elreyrestaurant.com

"This place was a dive," restaurateur Stephen Starr says of the Chestnut Street space that became El Rey. "That's why I liked it."

When Starr revamped the Midtown IV Diner into a "left-of-center" Mexican joint, he didn't want to lose that vibe. The restaurateur, long known for his polished, stage-set-perfect restaurants, wanted a touch of off-kilter authenticity for El Rey. For Starr, that meant keeping the Formica, Naugahyde, and faux stone and adding velvet Elvises and an obscure rockabilly soundtrack. (An attached bar, with its entrance on alley-like Ranstead Street, was even more of a dive. No more—Starr completely overhauled that portion of the building, creating the Ranstead Room, a dim, moody cocktail den.) A sign above the door announces, *"Esto cambiara su vida"*—"This will change your life."

Chef Dionicio Jimenez, who began his Philadelphia restaurant career as a dishwasher at Vetri and went on to earn rave reviews as the chef at Old City Mexican Xochitl, was tasked with creating

© STARR RESTAURANTS

a menu of traditional Mexican flavors inspired by his native Puebla, a charge which ensured that the new restaurant didn't compete with Starr's more mainstream Mexican restaurant El Vez, inspired by frozen blood-orange margaritas by the pitcher and a bicycle-turned-guacamole cart.

In this wacky environment, Jimenez serves up homey dishes like nopales (cactus), *esquites* (warm corn salad), and complex moles—and nachos piled high with black beans and chorizo, cheese and salsa, a must-have at any authentically Philadelphian Mexican restaurant.

CHILE EN NOGADA

"This recipe comes from Puebla. It is a really traditional dish in July and August when the peppers have a little more heat and especially in September," says El Rey chef Dionicio Jimenez. "September 16 is Mexican Independence Day, and Chile en Nogada—the parsley, pomegranate, and walnuts—represents the Mexican flag."

(SERVES 6)

4 tablespoons vegetable oil, divided

1 Spanish onion, chopped

2 cloves garlic, minced

½ cup dried apricot, diced

½ cup dried pineapple, diced

½ cup dried papaya, diced

½ cup golden raisins

2 bay leaves

1 cinnamon stick

1 pound ground beef

Kosher salt and black pepper, as needed

1 cup slivered almonds, toasted

4 ounces cream cheese

1 cup whole milk

1 cup chopped walnuts, divided

6 poblano peppers

⅓ cup flat-leaf parsley, chopped

1 pomegranate, seeds only

Preheat oven to 350°F.

In a sauté pan over medium heat, heat 3 tablespoons oil. Sauté onion and garlic until transparent. Add dried fruit, bay leaves, and cinnamon and sauté until warmed through, 2–3 minutes. Add ground beef and sauté until cooked through, 5–10 minutes. Season with salt and pepper. Stir in almonds. Remove from heat and allow to cool. Remove bay leaves and cinnamon.

In a blender, combine cream cheese, milk, and ⅔ cup walnuts. Season with salt and pepper. Blend until nogada sauce is smooth and creamy.

Place poblano peppers on a baking sheet and drizzle with remaining 1 tablespoon vegetable oil. Roast until skin comes off easily, 3–5 minutes. Use a clean dish towel to wipe skin off peppers. Cut a slit along the side of each pepper. Remove seeds and stuff with cooled beef mixture. Top stuffed peppers with nogada sauce. Garnish with parsley, pomegranate seeds, and remaining ⅓ cup walnuts in bands from left to right to resemble the Mexican flag.

PHILADELPHIA ICON: CHEESESTEAK

Humphrey Bogart, Oprah Winfrey, Bobby Flay, Kevin Bacon, and, of course, Sylvester Stallone—they have all paid homage to the Philadelphia cheesesteak. Forget the lightning rod and the Constitution, this simple sandwich with a slang all its own is Philly's best-known invention and our best ambassador.

The history of the cheesesteak starts at a hot dog cart in South Philly around 1930, when the owner, Pat, sold his own lunch of steak and onions on a roll to a hungry cabbie, and a Philadelphia icon was born.

But it was more than a decade before cheese and steak became one word. Again, Pat's King of Steaks gets the credit. Provolone was the original. Later Whiz would become the true king of steaks.

The 1960s brought Jim's and Geno's and those signed celebrity photos. Then came Steve's, Tony Luke's, Rick's, the obligatory politician photo ops (remember John Kerry and the Swiss cheese scandal?), the blessedly short-lived McCheesesteak, and the ongoing Philly argument: Who makes city's best cheesesteak?

© GETTY IMAGES

There are more than a thousand contenders for that title, but in terms of a traditional cheesesteak, John's Roast Pork on the border of Pennsport and Whitman since 1930 is the answer. (They also make the best roast pork sandwich, but that's another conversation) For new-school versions, restaurants have largely moved away from turning the classic into gauche appetizers (eggrolls, empanadas) and are instead making worthy and original additions to the cannon, like Michael Strauss's gooey, smoke-perfumed brisket cheesesteak at Mike's BBQ in East Passyunk and the Japanese cheesesteak staring rib-eye cooked in white miso broth at American Sardine Bar in Point Breeze.

ZaHav

Society Hill
237 St. James Place
(215) 625-8800
zahavrestaurant.com

Chef-owner Michael Solomonov struggles with how to define Zahav, his exuberant Society Hill restaurant: "I guess most people would call it modern Israeli. The irony is, there's nothing like this is Israel." Instead, the chef borrows from Israel's exotic pantry—filled with flavors from each culture that has called the region home—to create dishes that might more properly be called "modern Solomonov."

This is Israel through the eyes of an Israeli-born, Pittsburgh-raised, James Beard award–winning chef with an affection for culinary history and Korean fried chicken (the latter indulged by his more recent project, Federal Donuts). That Solo—as he is widely known—is cooking for an audience that may have never heard of *labneh,* kibbe, or *mujadara* hasn't dampened his enthusiasm or the restaurant's popularity: "Ten years ago, there wouldn't have been a Zahav, but people are more willing to try things now. We go through fifteen pounds of duck hearts a week." (Grilled with a carrot-turnip salad and onion puree.)

Solomonov and his business partner Steven Cook are also behind the all-day cafe K'Far (page 5), run by James Beard Rising Star award-winning Camille Cogswell, plus Abe Fisher, Goldie, Dizengoff, Laser Wolf, Merkaz, and Federal Donuts , but even with such a busy schedule you'll

© ALEXANDRA HAWKINS

© OLIVIA CACE

often find the chef at the bread station at Zahav, shoveling dimpled loaves of laffa in and out of the taboon while eyeballing the dining room. His and Cook's careful shepherding of Zahav is a main reason it won the James Beard Foundation's highest honors in 2019: best restaurant in the country.

CHICKEN FREEKEH

"I always start with the ingredient here and pick a culture there," says Zahav chef-owner Michael Solomonov. "This is a pretty simple rice pilaf with Amish chicken and flavors from Jordan and Egypt. The secret is the cinnamon."

(SERVES 4)

2 cups chicken stock

1 teaspoon black peppercorns

3 sprigs cilantro, stems and leaves separated

2 sticks cinnamon

2 boneless, skinless chicken breasts

Kosher salt and black pepper, as needed

2 tablespoons chicken fat or olive oil

2 tablespoons Spanish onion, diced

⅔ cup freekeh (available at Middle Eastern markets)

4 tablespoon slivered almonds, toasted

In a large saucepan over medium heat, bring chicken stock with peppercorns, cilantro stems, and cinnamon to a simmer. Season chicken breasts with salt and poach in simmering broth until cooked through, approximately 15 minutes. Remove the chicken and keep warm. Strain and reserve broth.

Warm chicken fat or olive oil in a medium sauté pan over medium heat. Add onion and cook until translucent, approximately 5 minutes. Season with salt. Add freekeh and cook over medium heat until the freekeh is fragrant and well-coated with the chicken fat or olive oil. Add half of reserved broth and continue to cook over medium heat, stirring constantly, until the liquid is fully absorbed. Repeat with remaining broth and cook until freekeh is al dente but not dry. Using two forks, shred chicken and fold into the freekeh, with toasted almonds and cilantro leaves. Season with salt and pepper.

WHOLE ROASTED LAMB SHOULDER WITH POMEGRANATE

"This was the first thing we ever made at Zahav. When it was still under construction, we had a seder at the restaurant," says Zahav chef-owner Michael Solomonov. "I had lamb shoulder around, and lamb and pomegranate are a classic. When we tried it, it was, 'Dude, we have to have this on the menu.'" **Note:** Lamb shoulder must be marinated for 2 days. Chickpeas must be soaked overnight.

(SERVES 4)

For the brine:

3 gallons water

6 cups kosher salt

1½ cups granulated sugar

1 pound garlic bulbs, bulbs cut in half

½ cup whole allspice

½ cup black peppercorns

½ cup fennel seeds

12 stems parsley

12 stems savory

For the lamb shoulder:

1 bone-in lamb shoulder (about 6 pounds)

4 cups dried chickpeas

1 teaspoon baking soda

4 cups pomegranate juice

4 cups water

2 sprigs mint

¼ cup flat-leaf parsley, roughly chopped

Special equipment: Charcoal grill

To prepare the brine: Combine all ingredients for the brine in a large saucepan over high heat. Bring to a boil. Remove from heat. Chill thoroughly before using.

To prepare the lamb shoulder: Using a fork, puncture lamb shoulder on all sides. Submerge lamb in brine for 48 hours, using a weight if necessary to keep lamb completely submerged.

Soak chickpeas in water with baking soda overnight.

Prepare a charcoal fire. Remove lamb from brine and pat dry. Grill lamb over indirect heat for about 45 minutes, being careful to avoid flare-ups from dripping fat.

Preheat oven to 350°F. Remove lamb from grill and place in a deep roasting pan. Drain chickpeas and rinse in cold water. Add chickpeas and pomegranate juice to roasting pan. Add water to just cover lamb. Cover roasting pan with a double layer of aluminum foil and place in oven. Braise lamb, basting meat with braising liquid once each hour until meat easily separates from the bone, about 5 hours.

Remove from oven and allow lamb to rest in braising liquid for 1 hour. Remove lamb from roasting pan and transfer braising liquid to a large saucepan. Simmer liquid over medium-high heat, skimming regularly to remove fat. When the braising liquid coats the back of a spoon and is reduced to about 4 cups, remove from heat. Add mint and parsley.

Preheat oven to 450°F. Return lamb to roasting pan and top with 1 cup braising liquid. Roast lamb until caramelized, about 5 minutes.

To serve: Remove lamb to a warm platter. Spoon reduced braising liquid and chickpeas on top of lamb. Serve immediately.

© ALEXANDRA HAWKINS

Amada

Old City
217–219 Chestnut Street
(215) 625-2450
amadarestaurant.com

Amada was Philadelphia's first taste of what was to come from chef-turned-restaurateur Jose Garces. Later there would be the rapid-fire openings (Distrito, page 17), the James Beard award, *The Next Iron Chef* victory, an expansion to other markets near (Atlantic City) and far (Palm Springs), a rash of closings, and an acquisition of the Garces Group. But before all those highs and lows, there was *tortilla Española* with saffron aioli, *piquillos rellenos* stuffed with tender crab, tender calamari seared *a la plancha,* and spicy *patatas bravas,* a luxe version of the equally addictive Tater Tot.

Amada, which opened in 2005, was the restaurant Garces had wanted to open since his days in culinary school, when he wrote a strikingly similar business plan for a class: a Spanish tapas restaurant that captured both traditional Iberian flavors—serrano ham, manchego, chorizo, spiked with olives, vinegars, citrus—and the vibe of the country's tapas bars. In Barcelona, *tapeo* is more than a culinary phenomenon; it's also a cultural one. In those crowded environs, tapas is as much about conversation as it is about *charcuteria.*

Garces's dream restaurant took on more details during a stint cooking in Andalusia, Spain. "The sangria barrels behind the bar, the hanging hams, the charcuterie slicer—all those elements transport me back to my days in Spain," says Garces, mentally walking through the stylish, evocative dining rooms.

"I want to transport Philadelphians. I want to give them a true, authentic Spanish experience, to give them that true festive feel of Spain," says Garces.

PAELLA VALENCIANA

"Start to finish the cook makes the paella at Amada to order," says Amada chef-owner Jose Garces. "I want it to be an authentic food experience for our customer. There are a few things here you wouldn't see in Spain, like the herb salad on top of the paella. It's not traditional, but it cuts the richness and gives the dish a freshness."

(SERVES 2)

3½ cups chicken broth

Pinch of saffron

Kosher salt and black pepper, as needed

1¼ cups Spanish onion, diced, divided

4 tablespoons extra-virgin olive oil, divided

2 tablespoons unsalted butter

1½ cups bomba rice

½ cup frozen peas

¼ cup piquillo peppers, julienned

3 ounces chorizo, diced

10 mussels

8 cherrystone clams or cockles

5 shrimp

2 tablespoons black olives, julienned

2 tablespoons flat-leaf parsley, chopped,
   plus ¼ cup whole flat-leaf parsley leaves

1 large shallot, minced

2 tablespoons lemon juice

1 teaspoon granulated sugar

¼ cup cherry tomatoes, cut in half

1 boneless, skinless chicken breast

1 lemon, cut into wedges

Preheat oven to 350°F.

In a saucepan over high heat, bring chicken broth
to a boil. Add pinch of saffron and season with salt.
Reduce heat and simmer until reduced to 1½ cups,
about 30 minutes.

In a paella pan or large cast-iron pan over medium-
high heat, sauté 1 cup onion in 2 tablespoons olive
oil and butter. In a large bowl, combine rice, saffron chicken broth, peas, piquillo peppers, chorizo,
mussels, clams or cockles, shrimp, black olives, and
chopped parsley. Season with salt. Transfer mixture
to pan. Bring to a boil and remove from heat. Cover
tightly with aluminum foil and cook in the oven for
25 minutes.

To prepare a vinaigrette, combine shallot, lemon
juice, olive oil, and sugar and whisk until sugar is
dissolved. Season with salt and pepper. In a small
bowl, combine whole parsley leaves, tomatoes, and
remaining ¼ cup onion. Toss with vinaigrette. Place
salad on top of paella.

Sear or grill chicken breast until cooked through.
Slice and place on top of paella. Squeeze 2 lemon
wedges over paella. Garnish with remaining lemon
wedges.

GOOD DOG BAR

Rittenhouse Square
224 South 15th Street
(215) 985-9600
gooddogbar.com

In 2018, Heather Gleeson and Dave Garry's Rittenhouse-area saloon, Good Dog, hired their first new chef in 14 years. Carolynn Angle, formerly of Standard Tap (page 99) in Northern Liberties for *16* years, took over for longtime chef Jessica O'Donnell. She's given the menu an update with dishes like fried smelts (a Standard Tap favorite) and grilled brie with strawberry-jalapeno jam, but there was no changing the legendary Good Dog Burger—a burger so memorable that *Philadelphia Inquirer* food critic Craig LaBan wrote a song about it

The secret to the Good Dog burger: Hidden within the hulking half-pound burger is a pungent core of molten Roquefort cheese

"Our goal was to have the best burger in Philly, but I don't remember exactly how the Good Dog burger came together," says O'Donnell. "Since we opened, I've seen a lot of recipes that put cheddar in the burger, but the blue cheese is much better because it melts so well and really cooks in with the meat."

"While I'm trying to expand the menu to broaden opinions about the food at Good Dog, I'm happy to continue the tradition of one of the original best burgers in the city," says Angle.

Garry estimates that the kitchen turns out an average of six hundred burgers a week. The Good Dog burger record is 952 burgers in one week—that's nearly five hundred pounds of beef and sixty pounds of cheese.

ROQUEFORT-STUFFED BURGER

"The biggest thing when you are cooking this burger is to get the grill good and hot. Just put the lid down and let it heat," says Good Dog Bar's former chef (and burger creator) Jessica O'Donnell. "Then put the burger on the counter and pound it to an inch thick, uniform all around so it will cook evenly."

(SERVES 4)

1 tablespoon unsalted butter

1 tablespoon olive oil

2 Spanish onions, sliced thin

Kosher salt and black pepper, as needed

1 tablespoon fresh thyme leaves, chopped

2 pounds 80 percent lean ground beef

4 ounces Roquefort cheese, cut into 4 pieces

4 brioche rolls, sliced in half and lightly toasted

Special equipment: Grill

In a sauté pan over medium-high heat, combine butter and olive oil. Season onion with salt and pepper. When butter is melted in the pan, add onions, stirring to coat onions with oil. Let sit until onions start to brown, about 20 minutes. Stir again and add

thyme. Reduce heat to low and simmer until liquid released by onions is almost dry and onions are caramelized.

Preheat grill to high. Roll ground beef into 4 loose balls. Pat balls into flat patties and place a piece of cheese in the center of each. Fold the edges of each patty up around the cheese and roll back into a ball with cheese in the center. Gently flatten each ball into a patty about 1-inch thick. Season both sides generously with salt and pepper. Grill to medium, about 6 minutes on each side. Place burger on bottom half of bun, top with caramelized onions and top of bun.

STANDARD TAP

Northern Liberties
901 North 2nd Street
(215) 238-0630
standardtap.com

Northern Liberties's Standard Tap was the city's first gastropub—before we even knew what that word meant and where exactly Northern Liberties was. The dimly lit bar, with a mix-tape-worthy jukebox and no televisions, with all local brews and a brusque chalkboard menu of smelts and duck confit, not nachos and potato skins, quickly became *the* standard.

"We wanted a place that was unpretentious, as easygoing as your favorite watering hole, that featured great local craft beer and uncompromisingly good food," says William Reed, who renovated and opened Standard Tap with Paul Kimport. "The renovations took three and a half years. That gave us a lot of time to hone in on exactly what we were building."

That was two decades ago.

Today the gastropub thrives in Philadelphia. (For a taste: N. 3rd, page 119; Good Dog Bar, page 96.) And once-quiet Northern Liberties is has matured into an established family neighborhood. Standard Tap expanded, and then expanded again. But, thankfully, little has changed behind the bar, which now features a slew of local taps, or in the dining room, whose tables are still populated by fried smelts, chicken pot pie, and duck confit salad, plus additions like Pennsylvania venison loin over creamy polenta and miso-smoked haddock with jammy eggs and sesame-ginger vinaigrette.

CHICKEN POT PIE

"This is like a really good chicken soup wrapped in puff pastry," says former Standard Tap chef Carolynn Angle. The dish is so popular, it has been on the menu for more almost 20years, but there's no special trick to making it at home. "It's all about letting the flavors develop slowly." **Note:** Chicken pot pie filling must be refrigerated overnight.

(SERVES 6)

For the pot pie:

1 roasting chicken

1 cup kosher salt

16 cups cold water

Additional kosher salt and black pepper, as needed

Vegetable oil, as needed

4 cups crimini mushrooms, cut into quarters

1 tablespoon garlic, chopped

3 cups celery, diced

3 cups carrots, diced

3 cups white onion, diced

Chicken stock, as needed (see "Step by Step," page 102)

2 tablespoons sage, chopped

1 cup unsalted butter, room temperature

1 cup quick-mixing flour

2 sheets puff pastry, defrosted

For the salad:

1 Granny Smith apple, peeled and chopped

1 large shallot, chopped

1 teaspoon fresh thyme leaves, chopped

1 tablespoon flat-leaf parsley, chopped

1 tablespoon Dijon mustard

1 cup apple cider vinegar

2 cups vegetable oil

Kosher salt and black pepper, as needed

1 head Bibb lettuce, chopped

¼ cup red onion, thinly sliced

1 cup grape tomatoes

To prepare the pot pie: In a container large enough to contain water and chicken, combine salt and water. Submerge chicken and brine for 1 hour. Remove chicken, rinse, and pat dry. Season with salt and pepper.

Preheat oven to 350°F. Cover chicken with foil and cook until legs and wings pull easily from body, about 1 hour. Remove from oven and allow to cool. Once cool, pick meat from bones. (Reserve bones, skin, and fat if making stock.)

In a large saucepan over medium heat, heat vegetable oil. Add mushrooms and cook until caramelized. Add garlic and season with salt and pepper. Add celery, carrots, and onions and cook until just tender.

Add chicken, season again with salt and pepper, and cook until all ingredients are heated through. Add chicken stock to cover. Bring to a boil and reduce to a simmer. Cook until liquid is dissolved by half. Add sage.

Using an electric mixer, whip butter until it has doubled in volume. Add flour and mix until fluffy.

Add butter-flour mixture to chicken mixture slowly, stirring until no flour is visible and mixture has a creamy appearance. Season with salt and pepper. Allow to cook completely. Refrigerate overnight.

Spray a large baking sheet with nonstick cooking spray. Cut each sheet of puff pastry into 6 even squares and place the squares on the baking sheet without touching. Add a heaping spoonful of chicken mixture into the middle of each square, piling mixture high, like a baseball. Stretch the remaining pastry squares over the mixture, bringing the edges of the top pastry to meet the edges of the bottom pastry. Press edges together tightly to seal and crimp corners. Refrigerate for 1 hour.

Preheat oven to 400°F. Bake until golden brown, about 30 minutes.

To prepare the salad: In a blender, combine apple, shallot, thyme, and parsley. Puree. Add mustard and apple cider vinegar and blend. While blending, slowly add oil to make vinaigrette. Season with salt and pepper. Toss ¼ cup of vinaigrette with lettuce, onion, and grape tomatoes. (Reserve remaining vinaigrette for another use.)

To serve: Serve chicken pot pies warm with salad.

STEP BY STEP: MAKING CHICKEN STOCK

"In a lot of dishes, stock is your flavor base. Your stock can make or break what you are doing," says former Standard Tap chef (and current Good Dog Bar, page 96, chef) Carolynn Angle. "The better your stock is, the better your end result will be." Angle's top stock-making tip: "Don't boil your stock too hard. It will get murky."

1. Roast
Chop 1 white onion, 2 large carrots, and ½ head of celery. Coat lightly with vegetable oil and roast in a 400°F oven until vegetables caramelize.

2. Simmer
In a large stock pot, combine bones and skin of a roasted chicken with 1 tablespoon black peppercorns, 4 bay leaves, 1 sprig thyme, and ½ cup parsley leaves. Add caramelized vegetables and cover ingredients with cold water. Bring stock to a boil, then reduce to a simmer. Simmer for at least 2 hours. The longer you simmer it, the more flavorful the stock will be.

© GETTY IMAGES

3. Skim
As the stock simmers, skim any fat that rises to the surface. When finished simmering, allow stock to rest, skimming off remaining fat. It is important to remove as much fat as possible.

4. Strain
Strain stock through a fine mesh strainer to remove remaining fat and solids.

5. Store
This method will make about 1 gallon of stock. Stock can be refrigerated or frozen in convenient-size portions.

PUMPKIN

Graduate Hospital
1713 South Street (215) 545-4448
pumpkinphilly.com

Ian Moroney and Hillary Bor live in the city's Graduate Hospital neighborhood. So when the couple decided to open their first restaurant in 2004, they choose the just-south-of-Rittenhouse neighborhood, not despite its dearth of fashionable restaurants, but because of it. Pumpkin, a deli-turned-BYOB, was just what the neighborhood was craving. Moroney, no stranger to creating big flavors in a small kitchen from his years working with his father in the original Little Fish, served up rustic dishes of lamb shanks and short ribs and Provençal fish stew.

"We just wanted to make this neighborhood nicer," says Moroney. Mission accomplished. In the years since Pumpkin opened, the rapidly gentrifying neighborhood has attracted residents and restaurants. And Moroney's cooking has changed along with the 'hood and the city's ever-growing restaurant scene. Refined has replaced rustic on the plate, though the dining experience remains neighborhood casual.

"I want the restaurant to thrive," says Moroney. "That means changing with the times and staying current and staying relevant."

One thing that isn't likely to go out of style: the restaurant's Sunday night prix fixe, fifteen years later still one of the best deals in town.

PHOTOS © NEAL SANTOS

STOUT-BRAISED SHORT RIBS WITH MAITAKE MUSHROOMS

"This dish started with the stout and the black garlic. We were just playing with those," says Pumpkin chef-owner Ian Moroney. The dish has a lot of steps, but don't let that intimidate you. "When you read a recipe—read it twice. Visualize it in your head. Literally picture every step," Moroney says, offering advice he follows. "Work slowly, work cleanly, and follow the method. It's not hard. It's not as hard as playing the guitar, anyway."

(SERVES 4)

For the short ribs:

4 short ribs, trimmed and tied by the butcher

Kosher salt and black pepper, as needed

½ cup bacon fat, divided

½ cup port

⅓ cup all-purpose flour

3 cups plus 2 tablespoons stout, divided

½ cup dried porcini mushrooms

4 sprigs thyme

2 bay leaves

1 tablespoon molasses

1½ teaspoons kosher salt

4 shallots, diced

10 cloves black garlic or white garlic

1 carrot, diced

1 rib celery, diced

4 cups beef stock

1 cup baby potatoes

For the mushrooms:

1 clove garlic, chopped

½ teaspoon kosher salt

¼ cup flat-leaf parsley, chopped

½ cup pancetta, diced

1¼ pounds royal trumpet or crimini mushrooms, cut in half

For the parsley puree:

3 cups flat-leaf parsley leaves

½ cup vegetable stock

⅓ teaspoon granulated sugar

Kosher salt, as needed

To prepare the short ribs: Preheat oven to 300°F. Bring short ribs to room temperature and season with salt and pepper. In a large, ovenproof saucepan over high heat, melt ¼ cup bacon fat. Sear short ribs until heavily caramelized on all sides, about 15 minutes. Remove ribs from pan and discard fat. Reduce heat to medium and add port to deglaze the pan, scraping up any browned bits. Sprinkle in flour and cook, stirring, about 5 minutes. Gradually stir in 3 cups beer until mixture is smooth. Add porcini, thyme, bay leaves, molasses, and salt.

In a sauté pan over medium-high heat, melt remaining ¼ cup bacon fat. Add shallots, garlic, carrot, and celery and sauté until lightly browned, about 10 minutes.

Transfer vegetables and short ribs to ovenproof pan and add beef stock to cover. Trim a piece of parchment paper to the size of the pan and rest on meat. Cover pan and transfer to oven. Cook until meat is fork tender, about 3 hours. Add potatoes and cook for 15 minutes.

Remove meat and potatoes from pan. Allow sauce to cool until fat rises, about 10 minutes. Skim fat. Discard thyme sprigs and bay leaves. Add remaining 2 tablespoons beer and season with salt and pepper. Return short ribs to sauce and keep warm over low heat.

To prepare the mushrooms: Mash garlic with salt. Add parsley to garlic mixture and roughly chop. In a large sauté pan over medium-high heat, cook pancetta until fat renders. Add mushrooms and cook until brown, about 10 minutes. Remove from heat and toss with parsley mixture.

To prepare the parsley puree: Fill a large saucepan with heavily salted water. Bring to a boil over high heat. Cook parsley leaves for 7 minutes. Strain parsley and plunge into ice water until cold. In a blender combine parsley and vegetable stock. Puree. Add sugar and season with salt. Pass through a strainer.

To serve: Untie short ribs and divide among four plates. Top with cooking sauce, parsley puree, and mushrooms.

Paesano's Philly Style

152 West Girard Avenue, (267) 886-9556
paesanosphillystyle.com

To an Italian, the word *paesano* means "villager." To chef Peter McAndrews, the definition is far more delicious. Paesano was the name that he and a fellow cook gave to their favorite late-night sandwich, a burger topped, quite improbably, with pancetta and garlic aioli and Gorgonzola dolce and french fries and a chefly drizzle of thirty-year-old balsamic vinegar. "It got the name Paesano's because you had to split it," says McAndrews. "You had to share it with a friend." So, when McAndrews opened his first sandwich shop, a small lunch counter across Girard Avenue from his first restaurant Modo Mio, to share his love of "in your face sandwiches" with the city, it was Paesano's Philly Style.

"Philly is a big sandwich town—cheesesteaks, roast pork, hoagies—but not a deep one," says McAndrews, who would indulge his sandwich addiction on shopping trips. "The sandwiches I got were always good, but they weren't great. I would bring them home and fix them. I wanted a sandwich that made a statement."

There seems to be no debate that McAndrews makes the best roast pork in the city, the meltingly tender Arista, layered with long hots, and the best hoagie in the city, the Daddy Wad, stuffed with five types of Italian cured meats. But it's McAndrews's own creations that have the biggest fans. The Paesano burger was retired in favor of the Paesano sandwich, equally worthy of the name: beef brisket topped with horseradish mayo and roasted tomatoes and pepperincino and sharp provolone and a fried egg.

LASAGNA BOLOGNESE

"We had lasagna Bolognese on the menu at his first restaurant. Modo Mio when we first opened. If we had some left over, I would fry it up, put an egg on top, and put it on leftover bread. We knew it was good," says Paesano's Philly Style chef-owner Peter McAndrews. "When Paesano's opened, it was a natural fit."

(SERVES 10)

For the Bolognese sauce:

½ cup extra-virgin olive oil

2 medium Spanish onions, diced

4 ribs celery, diced

2 carrots, diced

5 cloves garlic, diced

1 pound ground veal

1 pound ground pork

¼ pound pancetta, diced

¾ cup tomato paste

1 cup whole milk

1 cup red wine

1 teaspoon chopped rosemary

Kosher salt and black pepper, as needed

For the smoked mozzarella besciamella:

5 tablespoons unsalted butter

¼ cup all-purpose flour

3 cups whole milk

2 pounds shredded smoked mozzarella

2 tablespoons kosher salt

½ teaspoon grated nutmeg

For the lasagna:

1¼ pounds pasta dough

All-purpose flour, as needed

8 quarts water

2 tablespoons kosher salt

2 tablespoons extra-virgin olive oil

3½ cups prepared Bolognese sauce

8 ounces grated Parmesan cheese

1½ cups prepared smoked mozzarella besciamella

For serving:

Canola oil, as needed

1 cup all-purpose flour

15 large eggs, 5 eggs lightly beaten and 10 eggs fried

1½ cups bread crumbs

10 Italian rolls

Chopped rosemary, as needed

Special equipment: Thermometer

To prepare the Bolognese sauce: Heat oil in a saucepan over medium heat. Add onions, celery, carrots, and garlic and cook until translucent, but not browned. Add veal, pork, and pancetta. Increase heat to high and brown meat, stirring constantly. Add tomato paste, milk, wine, and rosemary. Bring to a boil and then reduce heat to simmer. Simmer for 1½ hours. Season with salt and pepper.

To prepare the smoked mozzarella besciamella: Melt butter in a saucepan over medium heat. Add flour and stir until smooth. Cook, stirring, until golden brown, 6–7 minutes.

Add milk, stirring constantly. Bring mixture to just under a boil and then slowly add mozzarella, stirring until fully incorporated. Add salt and nutmeg and remove from heat. Allow to cool to room temperature.

To prepare the lasagna: Divide the pasta dough into 4 portions. Roll each through the thinnest setting on a pasta machine and lay rolled pasta on a lightly floured surface to dry for 10 minutes. Cut the pasta into 5-inch squares and cover with a damp kitchen towel.

In a large saucepan over high heat, bring water to a boil. Add salt to water. Set up an ice bath and add olive oil to ice bath. Drop pasta into boiling water and cook until tender, about 1 minute. Transfer to the ice bath to cool, then drain on kitchen towels, laying the pasta flat.

Preheat oven to 375°F.

Assemble the lasagna in a 9 x 12-inch pan. Spread a layer of Bolognese sauce in pan. Sprinkle with Parmesan. Add a layer of pasta and top with besciamella. Repeat until all ingredients are used, finishing with a layer of pasta topped with besciamella and Parmesan. Bake until edges are browned and sauces are bubbling, about 45 minutes. Allow to cool, refrigerated, for 3 hours.

To serve: Fill a large, heavy-bottomed pan half full with oil. Over medium-high heat, heat oil to 350°F.

Cut lasagna into 10 pieces. Dredge lasagna pieces in flour, shaking off excess. Dip each piece of lasagna in egg, then dredge in bread crumbs, shaking off excess. Working in batches, fry lasagna in oil until crispy and golden brown, about 2 minutes.

Place fried lasagna in rolls. Top with remaining prepared besciamella, remaining prepared Bolognese sauce, and an over-easy egg. Garnish with rosemary.

THE DANDELION

Rittenhouse Square
124 South 18th Street
(215) 558-2500
thedandelionpub.com

The most striking thing about The Dandelion, from restaurateur Stephen Starr, is this: You hardly notice it there at the corner of 18th and Sansom. From the outside, the place doesn't exude Starr's typical panache, just a sense of quiet permanence, exactly what you expect in a classic English pub.

Starr installed a proper British accent in the kitchen—opening chef and ex-Londoner Robert Aikens' proper fish-and-chips endure—and some less-than-proper British decorations in the warren of rooms carved from two storefronts. (Read the tongue-in-cheek embroidery that fills the quaintest of the dining rooms.)

"The Dandelion was originally going to be a gastropub"—a solid, safe formula of creative bar food and craft beers that Philadelphia has enthusiastically embraced—"but no one had really done a true English pub," says Starr.

Among the English traditions Among those imported: bubble and squeak, pints of hand-pumped English bitters, and even bank holidays, when the kitchen turns out a traditional roast complete with Yorkshire pudding. (Also available on Sunday for those who can't name a bank holiday.)

FISH & CHIPS WITH TARTAR SAUCE

"This fish-and-chips recipe has been with me for years," says The Dandelion's former chef Robert Aikens. "I've tweaked it a bit. Generally when people make a fish batter, they do it with just flour and beer. I've put in cornstarch to make it a little crisper and baking soda to make it a little lighter. Make sure the dry ingredients are well sifted, and when you put it in the liquid, the batter should have a thick, thick, thick custard consistency."

(SERVES 4)

For the tartar sauce (makes about 5 cups):

4 large egg yolks

3 tablespoons Dijon mustard

3 tablespoons lemon juice

3 tablespoons white wine vinegar

1½ teaspoons kosher salt

¼ teaspoon black pepper

3 cups vegetable oil

6 tablespoons olive oil

½ cup gherkins, roughly chopped

½ cup capers, roughly chopped

½ cup finely shallots, chopped

4 tablespoons flat-leaf parsley, chopped

For the chips:

5 russet potatoes, peeled

8 cups vegetable oil

Sea salt, as needed

Special equipment: Thermometer

For the fish:

8 cups vegetable oil

1½ pounds cod, pin bones removed

Kosher salt and black pepper, as needed

3 cups plus 6 tablespoons cake flour

3 cups plus 6 tablespoons all-purpose flour

1 cup cornstarch

2½ tablespoons baking powder

2 tablespoons kosher salt

4½ teaspoons granulated sugar

3¾ cups beer

Special equipment: Thermometer

For serving:

1 lemon, cut into wedges

To prepare the tartar sauce: In a bowl, whisk together egg yolks, mustard, lemon juice, white wine vinegar, salt, and pepper. In a separate bowl, combine vegetable and olive oils. Slowly add oil to egg mixture, whisking constantly, to form mayonnaise. (Add a few drops of water if mayonnaise breaks.) Stir in gherkins, capers, and shallots. Add parsley just before serving.

To prepare the chips: Cut potatoes lengthwise in ½-inch-thick batons. Wash starch from potatoes with cold running water.

Bring a large saucepan of heavily salted water to a simmer. Simmer potatoes until they soften, but don't break at the edges, 10–12 minutes. Remove potatoes and allow to cool.

In a large, heavy-bottomed saucepan over medium-high heat, heat vegetable oil to 285°F. Add potatoes and cook until slightly colored and soft, about 5 minutes. Remove and drain on paper towels. Increase heat until oil reaches 355°F. Return potatoes to oil and fry until golden brown, about 4 minutes. Remove, drain, and season with salt.

To prepare the fish: Heat oil to 350°F in a large, heavy-bottomed saucepan over medium-high heat.

Cut cod into 4 portions. Dry fish well with paper towels and season with salt and pepper.

In a bowl large enough to fit cod portions, whisk together dry ingredients. Add beer and immediately dip fish in batter to coat. Gently place fish in hot oil, holding fish with tongs for a few seconds so batter seals. Fry until golden brown, 5–6 minutes. Remove fish from fryer and drain on paper towels. Season with salt.

To serve: Serve fish with 1 cup tartar sauce, chips, and lemon wedges.

Sabrina's Cafe

Five locations: Italian Market, Fairmount, University City, Wynnewood, and Collingswood
910 Christian Street, (215) 574-1599
1804 Callowhill Street, (215) 636-9061
227 North 34th Street, (215) 222-1022
50 East Wynnewood Road, (484) 412-8790
714 Haddon Avenue, (856) 214-0723
sabrinascafe.com

There are, certainly, other places to eat brunch in Philadelphia. But you wouldn't know that from the line that forms outside Sabrina's Cafe around 9 a.m. each Saturday and Sunday—rain or shine, August or February.

There are three tactics among the quirky cafe's regulars to deal with the wait, which can easily stretch to ninety minutes: Call ahead; although there are no reservations, the host will add your name to the growing list and estimate the wait time. Eat on a Tuesday at 2 p.m.; in 2011 the cafe finally started serving brunch all day. Or just enjoy it. There's always a coffee urn set up on the sidewalk, turning the sidewalk into an alfresco coffee shop where neighbors catch up while waiting for a table.

They are waiting for a peek at chef Lance Silverman's ever-changing blackboard of brunch specials (french toast filled with cream cheese and pineapple, fried trout with cheddar grits and poached eggs, pancakes topped with—believe it or not—strawberry pound cake) and consistent favorites like the Barking Chihuahua, the ultimate in breakfast burritos.

Owner Robert DeAbreu didn't expect to become the king of brunch when he opened the original Sabrina's—named after his newborn daughter—in South Philly in 2001. (The official name of the second location, opened in 2007, is Sabrina's Cafe & Spencer's Too, to be fair to his younger son.) The former Italian bakery had most recently been a short-lived breakfast and lunch spot, and as DeAbreu recalls, "I figured, I'm up early in the morning anyway."

SMOKED SALMON EGGS BENEDICT WITH HOME FRIES

"We change the brunch specials every two weeks. This is a favorite on the blackboard menu," says Sabrina's Cafe owner Robert DeAbreu. "It is a little different because the hollandaise has a little spice to it. Everything we do is like that. Everything we do has a little twist that makes it Sabrina's."

(SERVES 4)

For the hollandaise sauce:

8 large egg yolks

½ cup lemon juice

2 tablespoons hot sauce

3 tablespoons hot water

½ cup unsalted butter, melted

2 teaspoons kosher salt

2 teaspoons black pepper

1 teaspoon ground cayenne pepper

2 tablespoons tarragon, chopped

For the home fries:

3 pounds red bliss potatoes

2 cups vegetable oil, divided

2 white onions, julienned

2 tablespoons garlic, chopped

2 tablespoons kosher salt

2 tablespoons black pepper

Additional kosher salt and black pepper, as needed

For the poached eggs:

2 tablespoons white vinegar

8 large eggs

For the spinach:

2 tablespoons vegetable oil

2 pounds spinach leaves

1 teaspoon garlic, chopped

Kosher salt and black pepper, as needed

For serving:

4 English muffins, toasted

½ pound smoked salmon

To prepare the hollandaise sauce: Fill a saucepan with water and bring to a boil over high heat. In a metal bowl, combine egg yolks, lemon juice, hot sauce, and hot water. Place bowl over saucepan without touching boiling water. Whisk egg mixture rapidly, until it thickens and begins to set. Remove bowl from heat. While whisking, add melted butter. The mixture should be thick enough to coat the back of a spoon. If hollandaise becomes too thick, add a small amount of water. Add salt, pepper, cayenne, and tarragon. Keep warm until use.

To prepare the home fries: Place potatoes in a large saucepan. Add water to cover. Over medium-high heat, cook potatoes until fork tender. While potatoes cook, in a sauté pan over medium-high heat, heat 1 cup oil. Add onions, garlic, salt, and pepper and cook until onions are light brown. Drain onions.

Drain potatoes and allow to cool for 5–10 minutes. Cut potatoes in 1-inch cubes. In a sauté pan over medium high heat, heat remaining 1 cup oil. Fry potatoes until golden brown. Drain and combine with onions. Season with salt and pepper.

To prepare the poached eggs: Add vinegar to a large saucepan of boiling water. Crack eggs into water and poach eggs until set, about 4 minutes. (See "Step by Step," page 46.) Remove poached eggs from water with a slotted spoon.

To prepare the spinach: In a large sauté pan over medium-high heat, heat vegetable oil. Add spinach and garlic. Season with salt and pepper. Cook until spinach is wilted.

To serve: Divide English muffins between four plates. Place a poached egg on each English muffins. Top with spinach, smoked salmon, and hollandaise sauce. Serve with home fries.

PUMPKIN PANCAKES

"The inspiration for pumpkin pancakes came by accident," says Sabrina's Cafe chef Lance Silverman. "We had a can of pumpkin puree in the restaurant by accident, and we thought having another pancake option was a good idea. Always use a nonstick pan. A regular pan won't do the job."

(SERVES 4-6)

5 large eggs

8 cups milk

3 tablespoons pure vanilla extract

2½ cups pumpkin puree

2 cups brown sugar

1 cup granulated sugar

10 cups all-purpose flour

¼ cup baking powder

¼ cup baking soda

Pinch of kosher salt

2 tablespoons cinnamon

2 tablespoons ground allspice

2 tablespoons ground cloves

2 tablespoons pumpkin pie spice

1 tablespoon ground ginger

In a bowl, combine eggs, milk, vanilla, and pumpkin puree. In a separate bowl, combine all remaining ingredients. Add dry ingredients to wet ingredients, combining with a whisk until just combined. Batter will remain slightly lumpy.

Heat a nonstick pan over medium heat. Spoon ½ cup batter into the pan per pancake and cook until pancake starts to bubble around the edges, 30–45 seconds. Flip pancake and cook an additional 30–45 seconds. Repeat until batter is gone. Serve warm.

THE CALMELS FAMILY © KAIT PRIVITERA

Italian Market
1009 South 8th Street
(215) 965-8290
biboubyob.com

There used to be a vaunted French bistro in this tiny, unexpected space, slipped in between the Italian butchers and Mexican markets of 9th Street and the Vietnamese flavors of Washington Avenue. It was called Pif, and diners mourned its closing in 2007.

Now there is an even more celebrated French bistro—just thirty-two seats and a peekaboo kitchen—in the same small space, making an escargot and bone marrow statement in a neighborhood better known for ravioli, tacos al pastor, and pho. *Bienvenue a Bibou.*

Charlotte Calmels gracefully runs Bibou's simple peach-and-gray dining room, managing eager diners and a constantly ringing phone. In the small kitchen, her husband, Pierre, a Le Bec-Fin alum, turns out a menu of uncomplicated French dishes that remind diners not so much of the still-missed Pif as the ideal mom-and-pop bistro somewhere in France.

Calmels's confident flavors—*foie gras*-stuffed pig foot, juniper-scented sweet breads, crisp-skinned roasted duck—are a favorite among the city's wine lovers, who tote trophy wines for joyful dinners at the unfussy BYOB and make standing weekly reservations for the tough-to-get tables. Well-known wine expert Robert Parker is a fan, writing that Bibou "might be the best French bistro in the entire country," and, perhaps an even greater compliment, opening more than a dozen cellared wines at one dinner. And the warm, welcoming restaurant has earned raves from local and national food critics, including a spot on *GQ*'s 10 Best New Restaurants of the Year and a Best New Restaurant nomination from the James Beard Foundation.

ROASTED DUCK WITH POTATO CRIQUE & ASPARAGUS

"There is texture and color on this plate," says Bibou chef-owner Pierre Calmels. "We use a beautiful, tender duck. The sauce is rich and smooth. The asparagus brings freshness and crispness. And I love potatoes."

(SERVES 4)

For the potato crique:

2 Yukon Gold potatoes, peeled and grated

Kosher salt and black pepper, as needed

4 tablespoons extra-virgin olive oil, divided

3 teaspoons unsalted butter, divided

For the asparagus:

1 pound asparagus

1 tablespoon unsalted butter

Kosher salt, as needed

1 shallot, chopped

Chopped parsley, as needed

For the duck:

4 duck breasts, skin on

2 shallots, sliced

2 sprigs thyme

1 teaspoon black peppercorns, crushed

1 cup red wine

1 cup veal demi-glace (available at gourmet stores)

1 tablespoon unsalted butter

Kosher salt and black pepper, as needed

To prepare the potato crique: Preheat oven to 350°F.

Season potatoes with salt and pepper. In a 4-inch cast-iron pan over medium-high heat, heat 1 tablespoon olive oil. When hot, add one-quarter of potatoes, pressing to extract as much moisture as possible. Cook 30 seconds. Add 3¼-teaspoon pieces of butter to top of potatoes. Continue to cook until butter melts and potatoes start to brown. Flip potato and transfer to oven, cooking for 4–5 minutes.

Repeat with remaining ingredients.

To prepare the asparagus: Trim asparagus stems to remove the woody base. Cut asparagus tips, about 1½ inches long. Chop remaining asparagus.

In a sauté pan over medium heat, melt butter. Sauté asparagus tips for 2 minutes. Season with salt. Add chopped asparagus and shallots and continue cooking for 1 minute. Remove from heat and add parsley.

To prepare the duck: Sear duck breasts in a sauté pan over medium heat, skin side down, until crispy. Flip duck breast and cook 3–4 minutes. Remove duck breasts to a rack, skin side down. Discard all but 1 teaspoon duck fat from pan.

Using the same pan, over medium heat, sauté shallots until lightly browned. Add thyme and peppercorns. Cook for 2 minutes. Deglaze with wine and cook until wine reduces by one-third. Add demi-glace and bring to a simmer. Add butter. Strain sauce. Season with salt and pepper.

To serve: In a separate sauté pan, re-sear duck breast, skin side down, to crisp. Flip duck breast and reheat, if necessary. Slice duck breasts. Divide duck breast between four plates. Serve with potato crique and asparagus. Top with sauce.

N. 3rD

Northern Liberties
801 North 3rd Street
(215) 413-3666
norththird.com

It's hard to know what to expect at N. 3rd. An oversized eagle-shaped kite hangs from the ceiling, and skulls and shamrocks share the walls. Pierogies, quesadillas, spring rolls, and steak frites share the menu. And diners and their dogs often share the dining room.

This is a beer bar with a surprisingly good under-$25 wine list and a neighborhood pub as frequently praised for its "N. 3rd's Famous" wings and other bar noshes as for its list of nightly bistro-style specials from the imagination of chef Peter Dunmire, a veteran of Rouge (page 42), Blue Angel, and some of Philadelphia's other top kitchens, who relishes the opportunity to cook simple food well at laid-back N. 3rd.

"I like to keep it simple. I know it doesn't sound exciting, but too few restaurants focus on preparing food right. As for myself, I want to be part of the revitalization of salt and pepper," says Dunmire, who was a regular at N. 3rd before becoming its chef.

Owner Mark Bee, plumber-turned-restaurateur, first moved to Northern Liberties in the 1980s. "There was nothing here," he says. When Bee, who would go on to revitalize Spring Garden's Silk City Diner, opened N. 3rd in 2001, there wasn't much more.

Now Northern Liberties is a hot spot, and N. 3rd is a de facto living room for this quirky corner of the neighborhood—a place to watch the Phillies game and to watch short films from Philly's amateur filmmakers during the popular Tuesday night "Fancypants Cinema" screening.

ASIAN-SPICED TUNA BURGER

"I was thinking about an option on the menu for people who wanted a burger but didn't want red meat," says N. 3rd chef Peter Dunmire. "We had an ahi tuna entree that was made from the eye of the tuna, and I thought I could fashion a burger from the trimmings. We put the sandwich on the menu, and it became so popular that we were soon using the entire tuna loin to prepare the burger."

(SERVES 4)

For the tuna burger:

1½ pounds sushi-grade tuna trimmings

1 tablespoon ginger, finely chopped

1 tablespoon cilantro, chopped

1 tablespoon Sriracha or other hot sauce

1 teaspoon Dijon mustard

1 teaspoon white sesame seeds, toasted

2 tablespoons vegetable oil

Special equipment: 4-inch ring mold

For the salad:

½ cup white miso paste

¼ cup mirin

1-inch piece ginger, peeled

1 naval orange, peel and pith removed

1 cup vegetable oil

2 cups spring mix greens

½ cup mayonnaise

1 tablespoon wasabi paste

4 brioche hamburger buns, toasted

To prepare the tuna burger: Dice tuna. In a bowl, combine tuna, ginger, cilantro, hot sauce, mustard, and sesame seeds. Mix thoroughly by hand until well combined. Using a 4-inch ring mold, shape 4 patties, pressing tuna mixture together tightly.

In a nonstick sauté pan over medium heat, heat oil. Cook patties to rare, 1 minute on each side.

To prepare the salad: Combine miso paste, mirin, ginger, and orange in a blender. Blend until smooth. While blending, add vegetable oil to make dressing. Toss spring mix greens with 2 tablespoons of dressing. (Reserve remaining dressing for another use.)

To serve: In a bowl combine mayonnaise and wasabi paste. Spread wasabi mayonnaise on buns. Divide greens between buns. Place tuna burgers in buns.

PHOTOS © MARC WILLIAMS

Booker's Restaurant & Bar

Cedar Park
5021 Baltimore Avenue
(215) 883-0960
bookersrestaurantandbar.com

A longtime immigrant haven. A historic African-American stronghold. The city's eds-and-meds epicenter. West Philly is many things—among them, an outstanding place to eat. Saba Tedla has been a fixture in the neighborhood of Cedar Park since opening her health-focused Mediterranean cafe, Aksum, in 2011. Her follow-up, Booker's, is an American counterweight to the area's richness of Ethiopian, Eritrean, Senegalese, Vietnamese, Indian, and Middle Eastern restaurants. Located on the ground floor of two handsome, three-story, brick rowhomes, Booker's takes its name from Booker Wright, an African-American waiter in 1960s Mississippi who worked in a whites-only restaurant while also running his own restaurant for black diners. "I was pretty much moved by his life," Tedla told the *Philadelphia Tribune*.

© MARC WILLIAMS

Jambalaya, blackened catfish, and other soul and Southern staples flavor, but don't necessarily define, the menu. In Tedla's aim to make Booker's an inclusive neighborhood place, you can also get kickass crab cakes, a brawny grilled rib-eye with roasted shallot butter, and huevos rancheros. This easy mix has made Booker's a favorite for West Philly families, who gather in the teal-and-copper dining room for multi-generational dinners and brunches. The gleaming black-and-white marble bar, meanwhile, heats up at night with a deep whiskey list.

FRIED JERK CHICKEN & WAFFLES WITH PINEAPPLE BUTTER

When Booker's former executive chef Kurt Evans auditioned for owner Saba Tedla, he made a version of this dish with rabbit. While chicken made it to his eventual menu instead, the concept stayed the same: a mash-up of two classics, Caribbean jerk and chicken and waffles. The dish looks like the latter, "but then you get into it, and you get all that flavor," says Evans, whose sneaky jerk marinade involves Scotch Bonnets, ginger, allspice, thyme and dozen other aromatics. For Evans, who now divides his time between Philly, where he hosts the End Mass Incarceration dinner series, and Brooklyn, where he's the director of Drive Change, a non-profit where formerly incarcerated youth learn culinary and hospitality skills, activism is as much a part of his cooking as salt and spices. "It's important to me to be involved in community activism to create space for black people, create a meal that was curated by black people, and center black people in the conversation," he says. "I can't afford to be silent about issues that affect me or people that look like me."

(SERVES 2)

For the jerk marinade:

10 green onions, finely chopped

2 Scotch Bonnet chiles, stemmed and finely chopped

2 teaspoons thyme

2 tablespoons coconut oil

3 garlic cloves, chopped

½ cup coconut sugar

2 tablespoons smoked paprika

2 teaspoons ground ginger

2 teaspoons ground coriander

1 teaspoon chili powder

½ teaspoon ground allspice

½ teaspoon ground cinnamon

½ teaspoon ground cloves

½ teaspoon ground cumin

½ teaspoon ground nutmeg

½ tablespoon black pepper

1 teaspoon Morton's kosher salt

¼ cup orange juice

For the chicken:

4 whole chicken legs

1 cup yellow cornmeal

1 cup all-purpose flour

½ cup cornstarch

1 tablespoon smoked paprika

2 tablespoons Morton's kosher salt

2 tablespoons black pepper

Peanut oil, for frying

For the waffles:

2 cups all-purpose flour

4 tablespoons granulated sugar

4 teaspoons baking powder

½ teaspoons Morton's kosher salt

2 large eggs

1½ cups whole milk

6 tablespoons unsalted butter, melted

1 teaspoon vanilla extract

For the pineapple butter:

½ cup unsalted butter, softened

½ cup cream cheese, softened

½ cup confectioners' sugar

1 (8-ounce) can crushed pineapple, well drained

Maple syrup, for serving

Make the marinade. Bring a saucepot of water to a boil over medium-high heat and set up a bowl of ice water. Add the scallions, Scotch Bonnets, and thyme to the boiling water. Blanche for 1 minute, then immediately shock in the ice water. Strain off the scallion mixture and transfer it to a blender with the remaining marinade ingredients. Blend on high until the marinade comes together and is almost completely smooth. (The marinade can be made up to one day in advance.)

Add chicken to a medium mixing bowl with 1 cup of the marinade. Cover with plastic wrap and refrigerate for at least 4 and up to 24 hours.

After the chicken has marinated, combine the flour, cornmeal, cornstarch, paprika, salt, and pepper in a medium mixing bowl and whisk to combine. Line a sheet pan with wax paper. Working one piece at a time, dredge the chicken in the flour mixture to completely coat. Place the chicken on the prepared pan and refrigerate for 30 minutes before frying, which will ensure crispy skin.

Set a large pot of peanut oil over medium-high heat to 355°F. Alternately, set a deep fryer to that temperature.

To prepare the waffles: While the oil is heating and the chicken is chilling, make the waffles. Preheat a waffle iron. Combine the flour, sugar, baking powder, and salt in a large mixing bowl. In a separate small mixing bowl, whisk the milk and eggs together. Add the milk mixture, the butter, and vanilla to the dry ingredients and whisk to completely combine. Coat the inside of the waffle iron with nonstick spray.

Scoop half the batter into the iron and cook accordingly the manufacturer's directions until the waffle is crisp and golden-brown. Repeat for second waffle. Reserve the waffles in a warm oven until serving.

When the oil and chicken are ready, add the chicken two pieces at a time and cook for 12 minutes, turning if necessary, or until golden-brown all over. Remove the chicken and reserve on paper towels to absorb excess oil.

While the chicken is draining, make the pineapple butter. Combine all the ingredients in the bowl of a stand mixer fitted with paddle attachment and whip until the mixture is completely smooth. To serve, set each waffle on a plate and evenly spread the pineapple butter over it. Add two pieces of chicken to each waffle, drizzle with maple syrup, and serve.

Hungry Pigeon

Queen Village
743 South 4th Street
(215) 278-2736
hungrypigeon.com

Scott Schroeder is from Michigan, but he's been cooking here for so long (since 1995)––and has been so low-key influential—it's hard to remember a time before he was part of the Philly chef community. As the longtime chef at pioneering South Philadelphia Tap Room, he helped usher in the gastropub era back when we were still learning our IPAs from our ESBs, filling out his menu with headcheese tacos, fried chicken sticky with honey, and a totemic burger with (controversial) home-made ketchup. Schroeder was far from the only chef committed to using local, sustainably raised and farmed ingredients in the early Obama years, but he was the only one not making a big to-do about it and letting the high-quality ingredients speak for themselves—the same easygoing style that informs Hungry Pigeon, the restaurant he opened in 2016 after twelve years at SPTR.

"I realized that I had gone as far as I was going to go as a chef at South Philly Tap Room," says Schroeder. "I could have started looking for a new chef job, but that felt like a lateral move. I felt like ownership was a progression."

Schroeder's partner in Pigeon in Pat O'Malley, who moved back to Philly to join his old friend after seven and a half years running the robust bread and pastry program at New York's iconic Balthazar. The pair cooked together at *Pasion*, the dearly departed Center City ceviche specialist where, O'Malley admits, "At first we didn't really get along. Ultimately we realized we have somewhat similar upbringings and that our approach to food and what excites us were very aligned."

Together they created one of the most vital restaurants in town. As SPTR was on the vanguard of the gastropub trend, Hungry Pigeon was on the vanguard of the national movement toward all-day dining. Designed in partnership with the Schroeder's then-girlfriend now-wife, artist Maria Beddia (sister to Joe of Pizzeria Beddia, page 144), the open space invited diners to linger morning till night within its conservatory of butterscotch hardwood, sunny windows, and avian wallpaper. There's mobile of birdcages hovering over a communal table and a diner-style counter stacked with O'Malley's croissants, scones, and sticky buns. Ledges and windowsills hold fresh flowers and succulents procured from Southwest Philly farmer and florist Andrew Olson, husband of photographer and Lalo (page 135) owner Neal Santos. For one of the most populous cities in the country, Philly's restaurant community is remarkably small-town in scale, and the intersection of these relationships makes Hungry Pigeon feel like a clubhouse, one with an open-invitation policy and serious (but not self-serious) cooking.

CHICKEN SAUSAGE, EGG & CHEESE BREAKFAST SANDWICHES

"They're horrible now that they're mass-produced, but I used to love McDonald's Egg McMuffin," says Hungry Pigeon chef-owner Scott Schroeder. "This sandwich is a made-from-scratch version of the sausage-and-egg McMuffin," and it's become a daytime standby on the Hungry Pigeon menu, not to mention a microcosm of Schroeder's collaboration with co-chef and owner Pat O'Malley, who crafts the sandwich's peerless English muffin.

(SERVES 4)

For the starter:

35 ounces bread flour, divided

5¼ cups lukewarm water, divided

Combine 7 ounces of the flour and 1 cup plus 1 tablespoon of the water in a small glass bowl and mix together well with your hands in to a thick, lump-free batter. Scrape down the sides of the bowl with a rubber or silicone spatula and cover the bowl with a piece of cheesecloth. Set it aside in a cooler part of your kitchen for 2–3 days, at which point you should see bubbles starting to form on the top and sides of the bowl. There should be a dark "crust" on the surface and the starter should smell sour. At this point, you can proceed to the feeding schedule. If this has not happened then allow the starter to sit another day.

Discard about 80% of the starter. Add 5.6 ounces of the flour and ⅔ cup of the water to the starter bowl and mix together well with your hands in to a thick, lump-free batter. Scrape down the sides of the bowl with a rubber or silicone spatula and cover the bowl with a piece of cheesecloth. Set it aside in a cooler part of your kitchen. Repeat this process once a day for the next 4 days, keeping the time of day roughly consistent. After 4 days the starter will be strong, stable, and ready to use. (To keep it alive: When you are not planning on using your starter for a couple days, you should keep it in the refrigerator and bring it out and resume feedings when you wish to start producing again, it should come back after 1 or 2 feedings.)

For the English muffins:

1 tablespoon mature starter (see sidebar)

3½ tablespoons lukewarm water

5.3 ounces bread flour, divided

3¾ tablespoons whole milk

5.5 ounces all-purpose flour, divided

Scant ½ teaspoon instant yeast

½ cup water

2.8 ounces whole-wheat bread flour

1 teaspoon sea salt

1 cup clarified unsalted butter

2 cups yellow cornmeal

Two nights before you want to make the muffins, combine the mature starter, lukewarm water, and 1.8 ounces of the bread flour in a small mixing bowl, stir together, cover with cheesecloth, and reserve overnight at room temperature.

The following morning put together the poolish, which is the second "preferment" used in the English muffins. Slightly warm the whole milk to 75°F, then combine in a medium mixing bowl with 2 ounces of the all-purpose flour and instant yeast. Cover with plastic and set aside at room temperature for 3 hours.

Heat the water to 75°F, then combine it with the remaining bread flour, remaining all-purpose flour, and the whole-wheat bread flour in a large mixing bowl. Add the reserved starter and the poolish and mix until thoroughly combined and no dry patches remain. Sprinkle the sea salt over the dough, cover with plastic, and set aside at room temperature for 30 minutes. After the dough has rested, sprinkle some warm water over the top, then mix the salt thoroughly in to the dough by hand.

© NEAL SANTOS

Grease a large mixing bowl with cooking spray. Transfer the dough to the prepared bowl and cover with plastic wrap to "bulk proof" for 30 minutes. Uncover and pulling from the bottom of the dough, fold the dough onto itself. Recover, wait 30 minutes, and fold again. Repeat this process twice more at 30-minute intervals, then repeat it twice more at 60-minute intervals. At this point you'll have a dough that's been folded 6 times. Recover after the final fold and allow the dough to rest for 30 minutes.

Turn the dough out onto a sheet pan lined with a clean linen that has been generously sprinkled with cornmeal. Press the dough down into the pan in to a general rectangle shape, cover with plastic wrap, and place in the refrigerator for 8-10 hours or overnight.

After the dough has completed a second rise, turn it onto a work surface lightly sprinkled with more cornmeal. Roll it out to a thickness of about 1 inch. Cut out 4 muffins with a lightly floured biscuit cutter. Place the muffins on the same cornmeal-dusted pan, lightly cover with plastic or linen, and allow to proof for 30 minutes.

Preheat a cast-iron skillet over medium heat. Add the clarified butter and cook the muffins until they're golden and sound hollow when you tap them, about 3 minutes each side.

For the sausage patties:

12 ounces ground boneless skinless chicken thighs, chilled

1 tablespoon fresh sage, chopped

1 teaspoon Morton's kosher salt

½ teaspoon black pepper

1 small garlic clove, minced

3 tablespoons ice water

For the Dijonaise:

3 tablespoons mayonnaise

3 tablespoons smooth Dijon mustard

1½ tablespoons whole-grain Dijon mustard

¼ teaspoon honey

To build the sandwiches:

4 thick slices of jack cheese

4 large eggs

4 tablespoons unsalted butter

Kosher salt and black pepper, to taste

To prepare the Dijonaise: Combine all ingredients in a small mixing bowl and stir until completely incorporated. Reserve for plating.

To prepare the sausage patties: Combine all the ingredients except ice water in a medium mixing bowl and stir together with a wooden spoon. Add the ice water and mix very well until all the ingredients are completely incorporated. Divide the chicken mixture into 4 equal portions and shape into patties. Reserve for cooking.

Split the English muffins and toast in the toast oven or under the broiler. Add 1 slice of jack cheese to the bottom half of each muffin and return to toaster oven/broiler until barely melted. Spread about half a tablespoon of Dijonaise on each side of muffin and set aside.

Set a cast iron pan over medium-high heat with 1 tablespoon of butter. Once the butter is sizzling, add the sausage patties, cooking until crispy and well-done, about 1-1½ minutes per side. Place each patty on top of the cheese side of each English muffin.

Add 2-3 tablespoons of butter back to pan. Crack the 4 eggs into the pan and lightly season with salt and pepper. Allow them to cook until they are brown and crispy on the bottoms and around the edges, about 1½ minutes. brown. Flip the eggs and press them with a spatula to break the yolks. Cook for 10 seconds, then place on top of each sausage patty. Top with the other half of english muffin and serve immediately.

HARDENA

Newbold
1754 South Hicks Street
(215) 271-9442
hardenaphilly.com

The rice plate at Hardena is one of the best deals in Philadelphia. For the cost of an appetizer elsewhere, you get a Styrofoam frisbee heaped with perfectly steamed jasmine rice, which forms a cushion for the evocative Indonesian vegetables and proteins displayed behind glass on a steam table line-up. Point to what you want—crispy ginger-fried chicken, silky braised collards, aromatic beef rendang, its coconut gravy as dark as fancy chocolate—and Diana, Maylia, or Stephanie Widjojo, whose parents, Ena and Harry, opened Hardena way back in 2001, will cover your plate and pass it across the counter as the giant simmering stockpots in the galley kitchen just behind the buffet send up fragrant plumes that invade the fabric of your clothes and keep you thinking about Hardena long after your meal is done.

"The recipes are generational," Diana says. "We learned it from our mom, who learned from her mom. Her mom, Cicih, actually held a cooking school from her home so people would come and learn how to cook and bake. She saw the importance of cooking and providing sustenance for your family so she forced all her children to learn."

Ena, who's from Java, followed her mother's lessons and taught her daughters to cook. "It was always the idea that my sisters and I would take over the restaurant one day," Diana says. "My mother would have recurring dreams that the restaurant had a river of water flowing through it, which she believes is a good omen of rebirth because water brings an abundance of life and richness." Ena and Harry officially passed the torch to Diana and Maylia in 2017, about the time the women were named semi-finalists for the James Beard award for Best Chef Mid-Atlantic. "I was in disbelief that a small hole-in-the-wall place like ours could even be considered for something that prestigious."

Hardena has evolved under the second generation. The sisters have renovated, opened a seasonal location at the recently restored Cherry Street Pier, and established a strong social media presence. And it's not without challenges. "It is a bit difficult to explain to my parents why I take so much time doing social media, networking and charity events. Most of the time they think I'm playing around or not actually working. Sometimes we bicker but since we took over, our parents let us do whatever we think is best, as long as the recipes stay the same and we stick together as a family."

YELLOW CURRY WITH EGG & TOFU

This marigold-hued dish, a mainstay of Hardena's daily line-up, goes by the Indonesian name gule (curry) telor (egg) tahu (tofu). Its flavor is so vibrant and complex, it's hard to believe the foundational paste, a bouquet of powerful aromatics, comes together right in a food processor. This recipe is vegetarian, but the gule also pairs well with chicken and fish. Eliminate the eggs to make it vegan.

(SERVES 4-6)

For the curry paste:

½ cup yellow onions

½ cup shallots

1 cup ripe tomatoes, chopped

1 cup candlenut

2 red bell peppers

6 garlic cloves

Thai chiles to taste

1 inch ginger

1 tablespoon sweet paprika

1 tablespoon ground turmeric

For the curry:

5 eggs

5¼ cups grapeseed (or other neutral) oil, divided

4 blocks medium-firm tofu, well-drained and cut into quarters

1 stalk lemongrass, bruised with the back of a knife

1 teaspoon ground coriander

2 Indonesian bay leaves

5 makrut lime leaves

2 tablespoons soybean sauce

1 tablespoon kosher salt

2 pinches ground white pepper

2 tablespoon granulated sugar

1 cup coconut milk

1 cup coconut water

Water, as needed

For serving:

fried shallots

sambal

Make the curry paste by combining all the ingredients in a food processor and blending until completely smooth. Measure out 1 cup for this recipe and reserve the rest in the fridge up to 2 weeks or the freezer up to 2 months for a future use.

Fill a medium pot with cold water and add the eggs. Set the pot over high heat and bring to a boil. Cook for 7 minutes, then transfer the eggs to an ice bath. After resting for 5 minutes, carefully shell the eggs and set them aside.

Heat 5 cups of the oil in a large wok over high heat. Carefully add the tofu (the oil should completely cover it) and fry until the exterior is light golden brown, about 5 minutes. Remove the fried tofu with a slotted spoon and reserve on paper towels to absorb the excess oil.

Heat the remaining oil in large wok over high heat. When the oil is shimmering, add the coriander, bay leaves, and lime leaves and allow them to toast for 1 minute. Add in 1 cup of the curry paste, the soy bean sauce, salt, pepper, and sugar and sauté until the consistency thickens and the paste darkens. Add the coconut milk, coconut water, lemongrass, hard-boiled eggs, and fried tofu and simmer over medium heat for 10–15 minutes, adding water if the curry reduces too much and becomes too thick. Remove lemongrass and leaves and serve over jasmine rice topped with fried shallots and sambal.

© DANTE HINSON

LaLo

Old City
The Bourse
111 Independence Mall East
(No phone)
lalophilly.com

"Lutong bayay" means home cooking in Tagalog, "what our generation of Filipino-Americans grew up eating and how we came to understand our history and culture," says Neal Santos, one of the owners of Lalo, a Filipino restaurant in the Bourse, a historic Old City marketplace transformed in 2018 into a gleaming food hall. For Santos and his partners, Resa Mueller, Jillian Encarnacion, and chef Michael Cher, home cooking means crisp lumpia, house-made sausage with pickled green papaya, and of course, lechon (recipe follows), the crackly skinned, vinegary, braised and fried pork belly that serves as a road map for Spain's centuries of colonialist campaigns.

© LALO

Lalo got its start in 2015 as the pop-up series Pelago (short for archipelago). Santos, a prolific food photographer in Philly, had been shooting restaurants for over a decade, and "there was clearly something lacking to me, which was Filipino food. I didn't see our food represented or photographed, and I knew it should be a part of the fabric of this community." When the opportunity came to open a physical restaurant in the reborn Bourse, the partners moved quickly.

The address has a special meaning to Encarnacion, whose grandfather operated a shish kabob cart across the street in the 1980s, but being in the cradle of American democracy, right by Independence Hall, is meaningful for the whole Lalo team. Encarnacion, Mueller, and Santos are all first-generation American in their families, and the restaurant, Santos says, "is an opportunity to solidify the Filipino-American identity as something so historically and inherently American, right in the heart of Old City," where they're exposing their ancestral cuisine both to unfamiliar Philadelphians and to tourists from around the world.

LECHON KAWALI WITH GARLIC FRIED RICE AND TOMATO SALAD

Wherever the Spanish went in the sixteenth through nineteenth centuries, they brought pigs: Mexico, Cuba, Puerto Rico, and most definitely the Philippines. You can find a version of lechon (roasted suckling pig) in each of these countries; it's the national dish of the Philippines, the centerpiece of celebrations, holidays, and family gatherings. Lalo's version trades a whole hog for more manageable pork belly, infuses it with Southeast Asian aromatics like lemongrass and ginger, and serves it with garlicky fried rice and magenta onions pickled in a sugarcane vinegar brine. Though much of the cook time is passive, this recipe is a multi-day process to plan accordingly.

(SERVES 4)

For the pickled red onions:

1 large red onion (about 1 pound), thinly sliced

1 cup rice vinegar

1 cup sugarcane vinegar (substitute rice vinegar)

1 cup water

½ cup granulated sugar

¼ cup Diamond Crystal kosher salt

1 inch ginger, peeled

For the pork:

1 quart chicken stock

2–3 pound slab of skin-on pork belly,

1 large yellow onion, halved

1 head of garlic, halved lengthwise

3 inches ginger, sliced

1 star anise

1 stalk lemongrass, cut in 3-inch pieces

1 tablespoon black peppercorns

1 tablespoon annatto seed

3 bay leaves

1½ tablespoons Diamond Crystal kosher salt, plus more for serving

1 tablespoon granulated sugar

Vegetable oil, for frying

For the fried rice:

2 cups jasmine rice

3 cups water

2 tablespoons vegetable oil

4 garlic cloves, minced

Kosher salt, to taste

For the salad:

1 pint cherry tomatoes

1 teaspoon fish sauce

sliced scallions, for serving

Three days before serving, make the pickled red onions. Place the onion slices into a pickling vessel or jar, and bring the remaining ingredients to a boil in a medium pot. Let the brine cool to room temperature and pour it over the onions. Cover and refrigerate for 3 days.

One day before serving, preheat the oven to 400°F. Bring the stock up to a boil in a large pot over medium-high heat. Once boiling, add the belly skin-side up, followed by all of the remaining pork ingredients except the vegetable oil. Cover the pot and transfer to the oven. Braise the pork for 2 hours, remove the pot from the oven, and allow to cool to room temp. Remove the belly and pat it dry with paper towels. Discard the braising liquid. Wrap the belly in plastic wrap and refrigerate overnight.

While the pork is braising make the rice. Thoroughly rinse the rice in cool running water and strain. Combine the rinsed rice and 3 cups water in a medium pot and bring to a boil over medium-high heat. Reduce the heat to a low simmer and cover the pot. Cook for 10 minutes. Fluff the rice with a fork, transfer to an airtight container, and refrigerate overnight.

The day of serving, remove the pork belly from the refrigerator and slice it lengthwise 1-inch thick strips. Fill a deep skillet with at least 2 inches of vegetable oil and to 375°F. Carefully add the strips pork and fry for 5-7 minutes until crispy on all sides and skin begins to blister.

While the pork is frying, make the fried rice. Heat the oil in a frying pan over medium heat until shimmering. Add the garlic and saute until lightly golden. Add the refrigerated rice and stir occasionally until the rice is broken up, heated all the way through, and light brown, about 6–8 minutes. Season with salt to taste and transfer to a serving platter.

Remove the pork and drain on a plate lined with paper towels. Season with salt to taste and slice the strips across into roughly ½-inch cubes. Arrange the pork over the fried rice, the make the tomato salad by tossing the tomatoes, fish sauce, 1 cup of the pickled red onions, and a splash of pickling liquid together in a medium mixing bowl. Top the rice and pork with the tomato salad, garnish with scallions, and serve.

SOUTH PHILLY BARBACOA

East Passyunk
1140 South 9th Street
(215) 360-5282
southphillybarbacoa.com

It started in an apartment. Cristina Martinez and her husband Ben Miller were feeding the Mexican community in South Philly barbacoa, the dish of Martinez's home state of Toluca. Word got around about the lusciousness of her braised lamb tacos, and the couple launched a food truck in 2014 on the corner of 8th and Watkins, outside a Mexican bakery. Then word *really* got around. The truck led to a physical restaurant, South Philly Barbacoa, and an award from *Bon Appétit* naming it among the best new restaurants in the country. Then word really *really* got around.

"We did anticipate this success, because we have always applied our best efforts and integrity in what we do, and anything you work hard at with integrity and persistence will have success," says Martinez. She and Miller have not slowed down. In the span of three years, they took over Martinez's late son's restaurant, El Compadre, in the Italian Market; transitioned El Compadre into the new, larger home of South Philly Barbacoa; filmed an episode of David Chang's *Ugly Delicious*; filmed a episode of Netflix's *Chef's Table*, one of the most moving in the entire series; and relo-

cated South Philly Barbacoa down the street to an even larger location. The restaurant and its matriarch are internationally known—an astounding feat for a such a small place—but Martinez is one of the most humble Philadelphia chefs you'll meet. Perhaps because she knows that, as an undocumented worker, she can't take anything for granted.

© TED NGHIEM

That humbleness should not be confused with meekness, though. Martinez is an outspoken supporter of the rights of marginalized people. And her restaurant has become an incubator of meaningful political discussion, more than just a place to consume the city's most transcendent tacos. "We still have a vision of going deeper and doing more in our gastronomic lane and in organizing local political power through food," she says. "We try to guide the business by high spiritual principles of justice, compassion, equality and love."

CHICKEN MOLE TORTAS

While her lamb barbacoa recipe is too precious to divulge, Martinez is no one-trick pony. She's an outstanding baker, evidenced by the pillowy pan telera for this torta stuffed with braised chicken robed in mole poblano. "The secret is the coconut oil," Martinez says, which imparts a very subtle flavor and keeps the bread safe for vegan customers. This recipe makes way more rolls than you need, because "scaling it down would mess up the dough," but they can be frozen after the second rise then baked off as needed. (There are worse things than having a stash of ready-to-bake bread in your freezer.) For the sauce, Martinez's mother, Ines, is the mole queen. At South Philly Barbacoa, it's made by grinding over 20 ingredients on a stone mill. To save time without sacrificing results, Martinez suggests buying Hernán brand, which is available online or, if you're in Philly, at Fante's kitchenwares shop right up the street from the taqueria.

(SERVES 6)

4 teaspoons vegetable oil

8 cups 00 flour, divided, plus more for dusting

2 ounces fresh yeast, divided

1¼ cups water

2½ teaspoons table salt

3 tablespoons plus 1 teaspoon granulated sugar

½ cup coconut oil

4 garlic cloves

1 yellow onion, halved

3–2 pounds bone-in skin-on chicken thighs

14 ounces prepared mole poblano, Hernán brand preferred

Grease a large mixing bowl with the oil. Combine half the flour, half the yeast, and the water in the bowl and mix until incorporated. Cover the bowl with plastic and rest in the refrigerator for at least 2 hours and up to overnight. (This is the masa madre.)

Measure out 30 ounces of the masa madre and add it to the bowl of a stand mixer fitted with the dough hook attachment. Add the remaining flour and yeast, as well as the salt, sugar, and coconut oil, and mix on medium speed for 15 minutes.

Turn the dough out onto a floured surface and portion it into balls weighing about 1½ ounces each.

(The batch yields about 32 rolls.) Arrange the balls on floured sheet pans and allow to rise at room temperature for 2 hours.

After the first rise, shape the balls into rolls. Make two parallel indentations with a rolling pin on the surface of each roll to create the traditional pan telera shape. Allow them to rise at room temperature for 40 minutes. When the second rise is nearly complete, preheat the oven to 500°F and set a large pot of water with the garlic and onion over medium-high heat. At this point you can freeze all but 6 of the rolls for future baking.

Place the 6 rolls in the oven and bake for 15 minutes or until golden brown. Add the chicken to the boiling water, reduce heat to medium, and cook for 15 minutes. Remove the rolls from the oven and transfer to a cooling rack. Remove the chicken from the liquid and allow it to cool. Strain and reserve the stock. When the chicken is cool enough to handle, discard the skin and bones and shred the meat. Add the prepared mole to a large mixing bowl and add reserved stock a ¼ cup at a time until the mole has taken on the consistency of a thick gravy. Add the chicken and toss to coat in the mole. Split the rolls, distribute the chicken mole between them, and serve immediately.

TOWNSEND

Rittenhouse Square
2121 Walnut Street
(267) 639-3203
townsendphl.com

In the 1990s, the three-story building at 1623 East Passyunk was home to RoseLena's, a European-style cafe where wannabe Rosses and Rachels could sip mochas and Italian sodas on puffy armchairs. In 2009, as the kindling of a revitalization on Passyunk began to catch fire, the space became Michael's Cafe, a breakfast-and-lunch joint straddling the old neighborhood and the new, followed by Salt & Pepper and Sophia in quick succession. By the time Sophia closed, those early flames were a full-blown interno of activity on the Avenue, and a biochemist-turned-chef named Townsend "Tod" Wentz wanted in.

"I first took interest in East Passyunk when Lee Styer moved Fond from its original location and Joncarl Lachman was opening Noord. While I was looking for space, Chris Kearse signed the Will location and Nick Elmi opened Laurel in Fond's original spot," says Wentz. "With that many talented chefs joining the restaurants already on the Avenue, we felt it was a great community to be a part of." Coming from Cherry Street Tavern in Center City, Wentz signed a lease for the Sophia space, renovated the whole building (much of it himself), and opened his first restaurant, Townsend, with white-clothed dining rooms on two floors and bar in front that would become an incubator of local cocktail culture as well as a late-night industry magnet.

In the following years, Wentz has grown into a full-fledged restaurant group, with A Mano in Fairmount, Oloroso in Center City, and more projects in the works. (Wentz is allergic to sitting still.) But Townsend remains the home base—albeit in a new home in Rittenhouse Square where he continues to weave together a mastery of French technique, an eye for contemporary presentation, and just the right amount of borrowing from the global pantry. His sauces deserve their own cookbook: tarragon veal jus, curry vermouth cream, Pernod creme anglaise. You want to drink them from a Champagne coupe. "This is the food I was trained in while working with Jean-Marie Lacroix [at Lacroix at the Rittenhouse hotel]: unabashedly French, elegant, just 'so,' yet still comfortable and without pretense."

© NEAL SANTOS

COTE DE BOEUF FOR TWO WITH BASQUAISE PANZANELLA

At Townsend, chef-owner Tod Wentz shows a deft touch with delicate creatures like rabbits, scallops and snails, but when he decided to put on a steak on the menu, he went *big*. "I thought to myself, if I'm going to do beef, it's got to be côte de boeuf," Wentz says. "For the French, it's classic." At 32 ounces, this bone-in rib steak serves two or more, but it's so delicious you might want to keep it all to yourself.

For the Madeira jus:

2 pounds beef shanks

1 yellow onion, thickly sliced

2 carrots, roughly chopped

2 celery stalks, roughly chopped

2 pounds tomatoes, cored and roughly chopped

2 tablespoons tomato paste

1 tablespoon Dijon mustard

¼ cup sherry vinegar

½ cup plus 1 tablespoon Madeira, divided

1 quart veal stock

3 sprigs thyme

1 bay leaf

1 tablespoon black peppercorns

2 tablespoons unsalted butter

For the panzanella:

½ loaf sourdough bread, cubed

½ cup extra-virgin olive oil, divided

Kosher salt

Black pepper

1 yellow onion, thinly sliced

6 garlic cloves, thinly sliced

1 tablespoon sweet paprika

1 tablespoon Espelette pepper, plus more finishing

¼ cup Oloroso sherry

¼ cup plus 1 tablespoon sherry vinegar

4 roasted red bell peppers, peeled, seeded, and sliced into strips

3 sprigs thyme

1 pint cherry tomatoes, halved

1 English cucumber, peeled, seeded, and diced

½ red onion, diced

Maldon salt

For the steak:

1 (2)-pound dry-aged, bone-in rib-eye, trimmed and tied, at room temperature

Maldon salt

Kosher salt

Black pepper

2 tablespoons vegetable oil

2 garlic cloves, smashed

3 sprigs thyme

3 ounces unsalted butter

To prepare the jus: Set a large pan over medium-high heat. Add the olive oil and sear the beef shanks on both sides until browned, about 10-14 minutes. Add the vegetables and cook until slightly caramelized, about 10 minutes. Add the tomato paste and mustard cook until caramelized onto bottom of the pan, about 4 minutes. Deglaze with the vinegar and cook until evaporated. Add ½ cup of the Madeira and reduce by half. Add the thyme, bay leaf, and peppercorns and return the beef shanks to the pan. Add the veal stock, cover, and cook until shanks are fork-tender, about 2½ hours. Strain off the jus and reserve at room temperature until serving.

To prepare the panzanella: While the shanks are cooking, make the croutons for the panzanella. Set a large pan over medium-high heat. Add the bread cubes and half the olive oil and cook, stirring occasionally, until golden-brown all over, about 12 minutes. Remove from pan, season with salt and pepper, and reserve.

Make the peppers for the panzanella. Set a medium pan over medium heat and add the remaining olive oil and onions. Cook until the onions are translucent, about 7 minutes. Add the garlic and cook until tender, about 3 minutes. Add both paprika and Espelette pepper. Reduce the heat to low and cook until they begin sticking to the bottom of the pan. Deglaze with the sherry and cook until evaporated. Add ¼ cup of the vinegar and cook until evaporated. Add the roasted peppers and thyme. Season with salt to taste and continue to cook until until the onions and peppers are soft. Remove from heat and allow to cool completely.

To prepare the steak: Preheat the oven to 425°F. Liberally season the steak with both salts and pepper. Set a cast-iron skillet over high heat and allow it to preheat for 3 minutes. Add the vegetable oil and continue to preheat for 2 more minutes. Sear the

steak on one side for 7 minutes, then flip and transfer the skillet to the oven. Roast until the steak interior registers 122°F on an instant-read thermometer, about 12 minutes. Remove the skillet from the oven and set it over low heat on the stove. Add the garlic, thyme, and butter to the skillet and baste the steak until aromatic, about 3 minutes. Transfer the steak to a cooling rack and allow to rest for 8 minutes.

While the steak is resting, bring ½ cup of the reserved jus up to a simmer over medium heat. Add the Madeira and whisk in the butter off the heat. Reserve warm for serving. Meanwhile, finish the panzanella. Combine the reserved Basquaise peppers in a large mixing bowl with the reserved croutons, tomatoes, cucumbers, red onion, and the remaining sherry vinegar. Season with Espelette and salt to taste and toss to combine.

Carve the rested steak into thick slices and arrange on a serving platter with the panzanella. Drizzle the warm Madeira jus over the steak and serve immediately.

CRAVINGS: PIZZA

Philly wasn't always a great pizza town. There was a time, pre-2010, that our dearth of quality pies was a favorite citizen gripe right up there with dearth of quality parking. The first wave of solid pizzas landed shortly before this book was first published: Stella, Barbuzzo (page 9), Zavino, Osteria (page 82), et. al. following the Neapolitan-ish trend trickling down from New York (via Naples). The city's pizza scene (and pizza eaters) have undergone a long fermentation, if you will, and collectively we've come out that aging more opinionated about and more obsessed with hydration percentages, wheat sourcing and milling, and oven style. These are the pizzerias to visit now.

Pizzeria Beddia

1313 North Lee Street, Philadelphia, PA 19122
(267) 928-2256
pizzeriabeddia.com

Pizzaiolo: Joe Beddia

Neighborhood: Fishtown

Credentials: Joe Beddia's tiny and quirky original pizzeria was named the best in the country by *Bon Appétit* and closed in 2018; after a gap year he reopened with the Suraya (page 159) team as partners in a huge new space, expanded menu, and smart natural wine program.

Style: Round neo-New York

Pie to Try: #1 (tomatoes, mozzarella, Royer Mountain cheese) with pickled chiles

Angelo's Pizzeria

736 S 9th Street, Philadelphia, PA 19147

angelospizzeriasouthphiladelphia.com

Pizzaiolo: Danny DiGiampietro

Neighborhood: Bella Vista

Credentials: After operating an outstanding pizzeria of the same name in Haddonfield, New Jersey in relative obscurity, Danny DiGiampietro (an in-law to the famous Sarcone baking dynasty) relocated the shop to his native South Philly.

Style: New York round as default, with cameos by grandma and Sicilian pan

Pie to Try: Upside Down Jawn

Circles + Squares

2513 Tulip Street, Philadelpia, PA 19125

(215) 309-3342

Pizzaiolo: Daniel Gutter

Neighborhood: Kensington

Credentials: Daniel Gutter so enraptured the city's right-angle aficionados with his Pizza Gutt pop-up, it was only a matter of time before he spun-off into a permanent brick-and-mortar pizzeria.

Style: Originally crusty-edged Detroit, with recent additions of New York rounds

Pie to Try: Pepperoni

Square Pie

801 East Passyunk Avenue, Philadelphia, PA 19147

(215) 238-0615

squarepiephilly.com

Pizzaiolo: Gene Giuffi

Neighborhood: Bella Vista

Credentials: Philly fell in love with former New Yorker Gene Giuffi at his pork-centric BYOB, Cochon, but when the restaurant got lost in the shuffle of newer, shinier, more ambitious places, he turned it into a family-friendly, sit-down pizzeria that's become essential to the Bella Vista and Queen Village neighborhoods.

Style: Sicilian square

Pie to Try: Pancetta, rosemary potatoes leeks, and cream

Stina Pizzeria

1705 Synder Ave, Philadelphia, PA 19145

(215) 337-2455

stinapizzeria.com

Pizzaiolo: Bobby Saritsoglou

Neighborhood: Newbold

Credentials: Bobby Saritsoglou was the reason the early squares (and rest of the menu) at Santucci's in Bella Vista were so excellent. Now, finally, he has his own place to show off those skills, along with a whole Mediterannean/Middle Eastern menu.

Style: Wood-fired round

Pie to Try: Eggplant, kale, roasted garlic, za'atar, and brined cheese

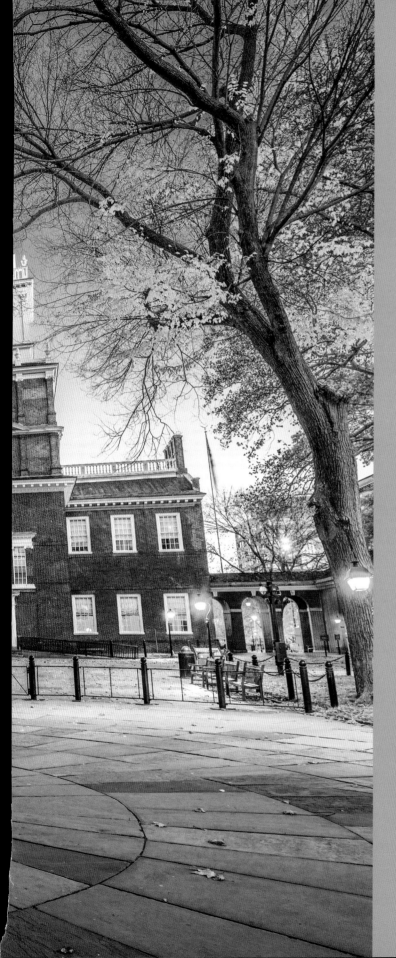

Desserts

This is a city with a sweet tooth. Water ice ranks with the soft pretzel and the roast pork sandwich for our caloric affection, and we lay claim to our own style of ice cream. Lancaster County is a bounty of produce, apple dumplings, and whoopee pies, and then there's the butter cake, oozing rich, dairy sweetness from Northeast Philly bakeries

We crave donuts (glazed in rose syrup and speckled with pistachios at Suraya, page 157) and cheesecake (with Mexican caramel at Lolita, page 155) after dinner, and carrot cake after breakfast—or perhaps *for* breakfast—at Honey's Sit 'n Eat (page 151).

For the eat-dessert-only crowd, there's city favorite Franklin Fountain (page 148), a re-creation of a classic soda fountain with, of course, Philadelphia-style ice cream. A fitting end to any meal.

FRANKLIN FOUNTAIN

Old City
116 Market Street
(215) 627-1899
franklinfountain.com

In their pressed white button-downs, stiff white aprons, and proper black bow ties, the Berley brothers—Eric, with his handlebar mustache, and Ryan, sleekly Brylcreemed—look as though they stepped directly out of a sepia photograph and into the modern-day Philadelphia restaurant scene.

Franklin Fountain, their Old City soda fountain, revives the days more than a century past when Philadelphia was known far and wide for the superiority of its ice cream, made with high-quality dairy products of Lancaster County and without eggs. But despite its ancient marble counters and fountain, Franklin Fountain doesn't have a one hundred-year history; when the brothers first saw the space, it was a niche bakery called Eroticakes.

"We saw the long, narrow space, the great original character, the tin ceiling, and the penny tile floor and thought 'soda fountain,'" says Ryan Berley. And there was that impressive marble bar, now the soda fountain counter, in the basement of the antiques mall in Lancaster County where their mother is a dealer. So began their transformation from antiques dealer (Ryan) and philosophy student (Eric) to soda jerks, and later, as the Franklin Fountain expanded, classic candy makers. "Historically, that's what a lot of soda fountains did in the winter," says Ryan Berley.

History provided the decor, the recipes for floats, phosphates, and rickeys, and the name, borrowed from Benjamin, whose original print shop was across the street. "He started out on Market Street, too," says Ryan Berley. "He was walking the same pavement we're walking."

HOT FUDGE SUNDAE

"A classic hot fudge sundae was one of the things we had to have on the menu when we opened," says Franklin Fountain owner Ryan Berley. "Our hot fudge sundae has Philadelphia-style vanilla ice cream, which makes it a local specialty. In the late nineteenth century, Philadelphia ice cream was well known nationally as being the best, and we lay claim to creating vanilla with bean specks, which proved that it was real vanilla." **Note:** Ice cream base must be chilled at least three hours.

(MAKES 4 SUNDAES)

For the ice cream:

1 vanilla bean

2 cups heavy cream

1 cup whole milk

1 cup granulated sugar

1¾ teaspoons Madagascar bourbon vanilla extract

¼ teaspoon Mexican vanilla extract

Special equipment: Ice cream maker

For the hot fudge (makes 5½ cups):

1⅛ cups granulated sugar

¼ cup light agave nectar

¼ cup water

½ cup unsalted butter

¾ cup whole milk

1¾ cups heavy cream

1 pound 60 percent cacao dark chocolate, broken
into small pieces

1 pound 72 percent cacao dark chocolate, broken
into small pieces

Special equipment: Thermometer

For serving:

Whipped cream (see "Step by Step," below)

4 maraschino cherries

To prepare the ice cream: Cut vanilla bean in half
lengthwise and scrape out seeds. In a large saucepan over medium heat, combine cream, milk, sugar,
vanilla bean seeds, and vanilla bean pod. Bring to a
simmer.

Remove from heat and briskly whisk until sugar dissolves. Refrigerate mixture until very cold, at least 3
hours and up to overnight. Remove vanilla bean and
discard. Stir in vanilla extracts.

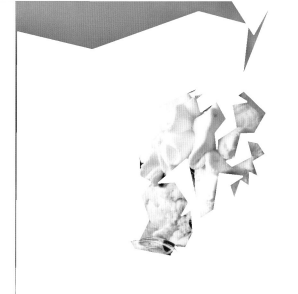
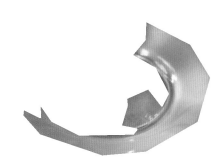

© FRANKLIN FOUNTAIN

STEP BY STEP: WHIPPING CREAM

"Whipping cream is ridiculously easy and incredibly tasty to do yourself," says former Franklin
Fountain pastry chef, Sara May. "Those canned whipped creams are pale imitations and are much
more expensive."

1. Chill
Start with a well-chilled metal bowl and well-chilled cream. A lower temperature will give more
volume to your whipped cream.

2. Combine
When ready to whip, combine 2 cups heavy cream, 2 tablespoons granulated sugar, and 1/2 teaspoon pure vanilla extract in the chilled bowl.

3. Whip
Using an electric mixer, or a whisk and some muscle, whip just until hard peaks form. Take care not
to overwhip.

4. Serve
Serve immediately with your favorite dessert.

Pour into an ice cream maker and process according to manufacturer's instructions. Serve immediately as a soft ice cream or freeze for a more solid treat.

To prepare the hot fudge: Bring sugar, agave, and water to a boil in a heavy-bottomed saucepan. Boil without stirring until mixture reaches 265°F. Add butter, milk, and cream. Whisk until butter is completely melted. Remove from heat and add chocolate, whisking continuously until fully incorporated.

Serve immediately or refrigerate for later use. To reheat, warm small batches in the microwave for 30-second intervals, stirring, until thoroughly heated.

To serve: Line the bottom of four parfait glasses with a little hot fudge and add 2 or 3 scoops of ice cream to each glass. Top each with more hot fudge and garnish with whipped cream and a maraschino cherry.

© FRANKLIN FOUNTAIN

HONEY'S SIT 'N EAT

Two locations:
Northern Liberties
800 North 4th Street, (215) 925-1150
Graduate Hospital
2102 South Street, (215) 732-5130
honeyssitneat.com

This is the reason Jeb Woody and his wife, Ellen Mogell, opened Honey's Sit 'n Eat: Jeb's Open Faced Biscuit Sandwich.

"I grew up in the South, and when I got up here, it was culture shock," says Woody. "I missed the simple things, the non-foodie aspect of going out." What Woody craved—what he ate every day at Honey's Sit 'n Eat long before it made the menu—was two fried eggs and two veggie sausages on a split biscuit smothered in cream gravy and, when Woody's eating, lots of sriracha. "Good ingredients and good food without paying for ego. That's why we opened this place."

Take Woody's Southern upbringing and add Mogell's Jewish one, plus Northern Liberties's come-as-you-are mentality and the Northeast's diner nostalgia, and you have the happy hodge-podge that is Honey's: hipster standing next to suburbanite in an hour-long brunch line, waiting for bagels and biscuits, *enfrijoladas,* tofu scramble, tuna melts, and a slice of one of those triple-decker cakes sitting on the lunch counter beneath diner-style domes. The formula was so success-ful it spawned a larger Honey's offshoot, in Graduate Hospital, that's arguably even more popular than the original.

The menu is, Woody says, "stuff we wanted to eat, the way we wanted to eat it," and the rustic, homey decor of the high-ceilinged space is a mix of salvage shop finds and pieces taken from Woody and Mogell's living room. "We like old stuff," Woody says, "and we wanted a place that looked like it had been there for a long time, a place that locals have been going to forever."

CARROT-PECAN CAKE WITH MAPLE-CREAM CHEESE ICING

"Our desserts are all the work of my wife and partner, Ellen Mogell," says Honey's Sit 'n Eat owner Jeb Woody. "One day she just decided we should have desserts. We sell a ton of them. We can hardly keep enough baked to keep them around. When there is a piece of cake left, I like to add a piece of cake to a milkshake."

(MAKES 1 CAKE)

4½ cups granulated sugar

1½ cups dark brown sugar

3 cups vegetable oil

11 large eggs

4½ cups flour

1½ tablespoons baking soda

½ tablespoon kosher salt

1 teaspoon cinnamon

1 teaspoon ground clove

Pinch of black pepper

6 cups (packed) grated carrots

2 cups pecans, chopped

1-inch piece ginger, grated

½ teaspoon pure vanilla extract

1 pound cream cheese, softened

1 cup unsalted butter, softened

1½ cups confectioners' sugar

½ teaspoon maple extract

2 cups walnuts, toasted and crushed

Preheat oven to 325°F. Grease two 10-inch round cake pans.

In a large bowl, combine sugar, brown sugar, and oil. With an electric mixer, beat until smooth and thick.

Add eggs one at a time, mixing until well combined. In a separate bowl, combine dry ingredients. Add dry ingredients to sugar mixture and mix until blended. Stir in carrots, pecans, ginger, and vanilla.

Divide batter between pans and bake for 50–60 minutes, rotating pans halfway through baking. Cool cakes in pans for 15 minutes, then transfer to racks to finish cooling.

Meanwhile, prepare maple–cream cheese icing. In a bowl, combine cream cheese, unsalted butter, confectioners' sugar, and maple extract. With an electric mixer, beat until fluffy.

Cut each cake in half horizontally. Stack layers, spreading icing between each layer and then frost cake with icing. Press walnuts into icing on sides of cake.

PHILADELPHIA ICON: WATER ICE

Almost every city claims its own icy concoction. Philadelphians demand the delicate texture balance that is water ice, more liquid than a classic scrape-and-eat Italian ice, its nearest cousin, but not enough to turn the spoonable treat into a 7-Eleven Slurpee.

The alchemy is no easy task—a combination of water, sugar, fruit juice, and fruit pieces, stirred as it freezes to reach the exact neither-here-nor-there consistency.

Perhaps that's why the city's chefs tackle ice cream-, gelato-, and liquid nitrogen-anything, leaving the water ice to the old-school South Philly experts. If you see water ice on a Philadelphia restaurant menu, chances are it's mixed with vodka or rum, the only improvement that can be made on

© STOCK CREATIONS/SHUTTERSTOCK.COM

classic flavors from John's, Pop's, Mancuso's, Italiano's, or the undisputed queen of the scene, Rita's. The Bensalem-born franchise now boasts locations from Massachusetts to Hawaii.

The Best Flavors at 5 Water Ice Stands, Ranked

1. Frosty, bittersweet, rind-speckled Lemon from Mancuco's cheese shop, 1902 East Passyunk Avenue

2. Cool, refreshing Iced Tea from Italiano's (Amaretto is a close second), 2551 South 12th Street

3. The seed-speckled seasonal Strawberry from John's, 701 Christian Street

4. Sweet and tangy, late-'90s nostalgia Mango from Pop's, 1337 West Oregon Avenue

5. Slushy, "creamy," and pastel green Mint Chip from Rita's, if you must, various locations

LOLITA

Washington Square West
106 South 13th Street
(215) 546-7100
lolitabyob.com

Philadelphia diners thought they knew Marcie Turney. She was the talent in the kitchen of Audrey Claire and Valanni, creating some of the city's favorite modern Mediterranean dishes. Then, in 2004, she opened her own restaurant—surprise!—Mexican-influenced Lolita.

"We love to eat Mexican food," says Turney, who owns the restaurant with her partner, Valerie Safran. "And every time we traveled to Chicago, we would make reservations at Rick Bayless's restaurants and think that there was no one doing anything like that here."

The instantly hip BYOB—or BYO tequila, the better to spike the restaurant's delicious margarita mixes—deftly combined Mexican flavors with New American dishes. The beet and goat cheeses salad was reimagined with mango, plantains, and a serrano-lime vinaigrette; cheesecake met cajeta caramel and the spice of ancho.

© NEAL SANTOS

Turney and Safran, who also own the home store Open House, which opened on 13th Street a year and a half before Lolita, followed their popular Mexican restaurant with gourmet-to-go Grocery. Then chocolate shop Verde; a return to Marcie's Mediterranean dishes with Barbuzzo (page 9), Jamonera, and Little Nonna's; and Bud & Marilyn's, the American supperclub inspired by her Wisconsinite grandparents After becoming the queens of 13th Street, Marcie and Val are turning their attention to East Passyunk Avenue and, most unexpectedly, the airport, where a Bud & Marilyn's will feed flyers later this year.

Turney says, "We just keep asking ourselves: What does this neighborhood need? What does every great neighborhood need?"

CHEESECAKE WITH CAJETA CARAMEL

"This recipe was a mistake," says Lolita chef-owner Marcie Turney. "This has been on the menu since we started, but we were making a much denser cheesecake. Then a cook mixed the cream cheese for too long, and it was so light that we kept doing it that way. The ancho chile in the

chocolate cookie crumbles gives a little bit of heat. When they first saw that, people thought we were crazy."

(MAKES 24 CUPCAKES)

For the cajeta caramel:

1 cup heavy cream

½ teaspoon pure vanilla extract

½ teaspoon kosher salt

¼ cup unsalted butter

2 tablespoons light corn syrup

½ cup granulated sugar

½–1 tablespoon water

3 tablespoons young goat cheese

For the cupcakes:

1 cup ground dark chocolate wafers
   (Lolita uses Oreos)

⅛ teaspoon ground ancho chile

4 tablespoons unsalted butter, melted

1½ cups cream cheese, at room temperature

8 tablespoons granulated sugar, divided

1½ teaspoons pure vanilla extract, divided

2 large eggs

1 cup sour cream

For serving:

1½ cups toasted pecans

Whipped cream, as needed (see "Step by Step,"
   page 149)

To prepare the cajeta caramel: Combine cream, vanilla, and salt in a small saucepan over medium heat. Bring to a simmer. Add butter and remove from heat.

In a large saucepan, combine corn syrup and sugar. Add enough water to make the mixture look "sandy." Over medium heat bring sugar mixture to a boil, cooking without stirring and occasionally

swirling the pan to mix. Cook until caramel is a deep amber color. Remove from heat and immediately add cream mixture. Be careful as it will steam and spit. Whisk to combine. Add goat cheese and whisk until smooth. Pour through a strainer.

To prepare the cupcakes: Preheat oven to 375°F. Line muffin pans with cupcake wrappers and spray inside of wrappers with nonstick spray.

In a small bowl, mix ground wafers, ancho chile powder, and butter until crumbs are evenly moistened. Place 1 tablespoon crust into each cupcake wrapper and pat down with the back of a spoon. Refrigerate 15 minutes.

In a large bowl use an electric mixer to beat the cream cheese until light and creamy, about 5 minutes. Add 6 tablespoons sugar and ½ teaspoon vanilla and beat until blended. Add eggs one at a time and beat until just smooth, scraping down the sides and bottom of the bowl so that all ingredients are thoroughly mixed.

Pour cream cheese mixture into cupcake wrappers, leaving one-quarter inch of space at top. Bake until cheesecake is firm, but not browned, and the center is set, 25–30 minutes. Remove from oven and cool for 30 minutes. (Cheesecake will fall slightly as it cools.)

In a small bowl, mix sour cream, remaining 2 tablespoons sugar, and remaining 1 teaspoon vanilla. Pour over cupcakes and bake 10 minutes. Transfer to rack to cool.

To serve: Serve cheesecakes at room temperature topped with cajeta caramel, toasted pecans, and whipped cream.

PERFECT PAIRING

Death Rides a Pale Horse
Franklin Mortgage

"Fino sherry is nutty, Aperol brings citrus, and bourbon brings spice," says former Franklin bartender Colin Shearn. "Spice, nuts, and citrus is a classic combination, one that is found in a lot of desserts, too. This will pair well with them—or it can be enjoyed on its own as we serve it at the bar."

(SERVES 1)

For the demerara sugar syrup (makes about 1 cup):

2 cups demerara sugar

1 cup water

For the cocktail:

1½ ounces fino sherry

½ ounce Aperol

½ ounce Old Grand-Dad 114 proof bourbon

1 teaspoon demerara sugar syrup

(recipe follows)

2 dashes orange bitters

1 dash absinthe

Ice

To prepare the demerara sugar syrup: In a small saucepan over low heat, combine sugar and water. Simmer until sugar dissolves. Allow to cool.

To prepare the cocktail: Stir all ingredients over ice until well chilled. Strain into a chilled cocktail glass.

The Franklin Mortgage & Investment Co.

112 South 18th Street
(215) 467-3277
thefranklinbar.com

suraya

Fishtown
1528 Frankford Avenue
(215) 302-1900
surayaphilly.com

Philly diners weren't exactly clamoring for a
Lebanese market and cafe when Suraya was
announced in 2017. But the partners behind
the place, Greg Root and chef Nick Kennedy
of Root, Cafe La Maude's Nathalie Richan, and
her brother, prolific Fishtown developer Roland
Kassis, knew something we didn't. "It was a
big vision, but we saw how unique and special
Suraya could be," says Root.

When Suraya opened on Frankford Avenue,
the city was instantly smitten with its good
looks. Restaurants just don't *look* like this in
Philadelphia: sprawling and lofty, with three
separate seating venues, from the bustling cafe/
grocery up front to the open kitchen-anchored
dining room to the tranquil rear garden that
resembles something out of a Relais & Cha-
teaux riad in Marrakech. (The benefits to having a real estate kingpin as partner...) Says Root,
"You get a lot on one space."

Suraya's appeal is skin-deep as well, thanks
to Kennedy's able handling of Richan and
Kassis' family recipes. His kitchen fires all day,
from labneh-slicked manoushe and omelets

© BREANNE FURLONG FOR 646 COMMUNICATIONS

so loaded with herbs they're green in the morning to cinnamon-spiced lamb sausage and grilled
black bass over turmeric rice at night. Many people think of the cooking here as Zahav (page 89)
Lite––the restaurants share a Levantine pantry and passion for grilling over smoldering coals––but
Suraya is so thrilling in its own right it's become nearly as hard to land a dinner reservation here.

ROSE & PISTACHIO CRULLER

"It was new and it was challenging," Suraya pastry chef James Matty says of getting thrown into
the deep end of Middle Eastern desserts. "Nathalie and her mother did a ton of cooking for us to
show us the ropes," ropes he now handles like an Olympic gymnast. Step into Suraya, and the riot
of confections behind glass at the pastry counter will throw you into paradox of choice: Do you get

the jalouise, with date-and-apple filling peeking through its latticed top, or the cardamom kouign aman? The seven-spice coffee cake or the tahina-mulberry Linzer? In an ideal world, you get them all, but if your pastry budget limits you to just one, make it the peerless cruller lacquered in rose-and-pistachio glaze. Matty says this donut is the MVP of pastry roster.

(MAKES 6-8 DONUTS)

For the dough

½ cup water

½ cup whole milk

5 tablespoons unsalted butter

1 tablespoon granulated sugar

1¾ cups bread flour, sifted

5 large eggs

Vegetable oil, for frying

For the glaze

1 (16-ounce) box confectioners' sugar

½ cup whole milk

1 tablespoon honey

1 tablespoon unsalted butter

½ teaspoon rose water

Chopped shelled pistachios, for topping

Make the dough by combining the water, milk, butter, sugar, and salt to a boil in a large saucepot. When boiling, add the flour and continue to cook, continuously stirring until the mixture forms into a ball and a thin film forms on the bottom of the pan, approximately 30 seconds.

Transfer to the mixture to the bowl of a stand mixer fitted with the paddle attachment and mix on medium speed. Add the eggs one at a time, scraping between each addition until a smooth and thick batter forms.

© BREANNE FURLONG FOR 646 COMMUNICATIONS

Transfer the batter to a pastry bag fitted with a ½-inch star tip. Line a cutting board or work surface with parchment paper and liberally brush it with vegetable oil. Pipe 6-8 four-inch circles onto the parchment. Cut the parchment to separate the crullers and allow them to rest for 15 minutes.

While the crullers are resting, heat a large pot of vegetable oil to 375°F. While the oil is coming to temperature, make the glaze. Add the confectioners' sugar to a mixing bowl. Bring the milk, butter, and honey to a boil in a saucepot over medium-high heat. (If the mixture looks slightly curdled, don't worry; that's normal.). Slowly add the milk mixture to the sugar, stirring until a thick glaze forms.

Cover the surface of the glaze with plastic wrap and reserve at room temperature.

Fry the crullers by lowering them into the hot oil batter side-down and peeling off the paper. (A 10-inch pot will accommodate about three crullers at a time.) Cook for 5 minutes and carefully flip. Cook on the opposite sides for 5 minutes. Carefully flip again and cook 1 additional minute on the first sides. Remove the crullers from the oil and drain for a moment on a cooling rack. Dip both sides of each cruller in the rose glaze while hot and transfer back to the cooling rack. Top each cruller with crushed pistachios and serve once the glaze sets, about 5 minutes.

Terrain Garden Cafe

Glen Mills
914 Baltimore Pike
610-459-3060
shopterrain.com/pages/glen-mills-restaurant

Urban Outfitters' parent company made huge news when it bought (then sold off or closed) most of Marc Vetri's (page 63) portfolio, but it wasn't the first time URBN had gotten into the restaurant business. In 2008, the company opened Terrain, an impeccably styled Chester County shangri-la of shade trees, heirloom seeds, exotic flowers, and faux-rustic housewares for folks with multiple houses to decorate. Concrete-afflicted Philadelphians take the ride down 95 on nice days just

© LARISSA CROSSLEY

wander the sprawling nursery's orderly rows of Japanese maples and eruptions of lavender, making an afternoon of it by back-ending the leaf peeping with a visit to Terrain's storybook-like Garden Cafe.

Housed in a vintage Victorian greenhouse overlooking the plant life, the Cafe serves brunch and dinner, pastries and coffee, with a focus on local purveyors. The restaurant shines during dessert, where pastry chef Rob Toland turns out confections with such intelligence and elan, you wonder why he's not running the dessert program at some fancy restaurant in Center City. "What made me fall in love with terrain was how spacious the site is," he says. "It's unlike any place I've ever worked because you feel so close to nature. It's so easy to stay inspired because of our lush, green environment."

BLACKBERRY ELDERFLOWER TART WITH LEMON POPPY ICE CREAM

This tart is inspired by Vernick (page 31), says pastry chef Rob Toland. "Quite a few years ago, when Vernick first opened there was a blueberry pie with vanilla gelato that I still think about to this day. Our blackberry tart may not resemble it in any way but, for me, it's a direct inspiration."

(MAKES ONE 8-INCH TART)

For the crust:

3¼ tablespoons almond flour

⅓ teaspoon Diamond Crystal kosher salt

1½ cups plus 3 tablespoons all-purpose flour, plus more for dusting

8½ tablespoons unsalted butter

¾ cup confectioners' sugar

½ teaspoon vanilla bean paste

3 large egg yolks

For the ice cream:

3 cups whole milk

1 cup heavy cream

1½ cup granulated sugar

12 large egg yolks

5 lemons

2 tablespoons poppy seeds

For the granola:

3 cups rolled oats

1 cup golden raisins

½ cup almonds

¼ cup sunflower seeds

½ cup honey

½ cup light brown sugar

½ cup sunflower oil

1 teaspoon Diamond Crystal kosher salt

For the filling:

4 cups blackberries

½ cup granulated sugar

2½ tablespoons cornstarch

¼ cup water

1 tablespoon elderflower liqueur, such as
   St. Germain

To prepare the crust: Sift together almond flour, salt, and all-purpose flour together into a large mixing bowl and set aside. Add the butter and sugar to the bowl of a stand mixer fitted with the paddle attachment and cream together on medium speed, scraping down the sides of the bowl periodically, until light and fluffy, about 10 minutes. Add the yolks one at a time, being sure to fully incorporate each addition into the butter. Scrape the sides of the bowl, add all of the flour mixture and mix until just incorporated. Finish mixing the dough by hand to eliminate any remaining dry spots. Turn the dough

out onto a piece of plastic wrap and shape it into a flat circle. Wrap the dough and refrigerate for 1 hour.

To prepare the ice cream: Add the milk, sugar, and yolks to a medium stainless-steel pot set over medium heat and bring to 160°F, whisking constantly to avoid scorching. Switch to a rubber or silicone spatula and continue to stir and scrape the bottom of the pot until the mixture reaches 180°F. Strain the ice cream base into a separate container, add the lemon zest and poppy seeds to the base, and chill for at least 12 hours. Process the ice cream according to the manufacturer's instructions and reserve frozen until ready to use.

Unwrap the chilled dough and roll it out onto a floured surface to roughly ¼-inch thickness. Gently drape the dough over an 8-inch tart shell, pressing firmly into the corners. Chill, uncovered, for one hour.

To prepare the granola: Preheat the oven to 325°F. Combine oats, raisins, almonds, and seeds in a medium mixing bowl. Whisk together the honey, brown sugar, salt and oil in a small mixing bowl. Add the honey mixture to the oat mixture, stir together to combine, and spread on a sheet pan in a thin, even layer. Bake the mixture for 20 minutes or until golden brown. Remove the granola from the oven; it will firm up and become crunchy when completely cool. Break up the granola into pieces when it's cool enough to handle and reserve in an airtight container for plating.

Remove the tart shell from the refrigerator and increase the oven to 350°F. Trim the excess dough off the edges of the shell, using to patch tears if necessary. Cover the tart shell with a piece of parchment large enough to leave a 2-inch border on all sides and fill the shell with pie weights or dried beans. Blind-bake for 15 minutes, remove the weights and parchment paper, and continue to bake until the crust is light golden brown throughout, 5-10 minutes. Cool completely.

To prepare the filling: While the shell is cooling, make the filling. Combine the blackberries, sugar, and cornstarch in a medium sauce pot and allow to macerate for 5-10 minutes. Add the water and bring the berry mixture to a boil, then turn down to a simmer, and cook until the berries become thick and jammy, about 5 minutes. Stir in the elderflower liqueur and allow to cool completely before filling the tart.

To serve: Spread the filling in an even layer in the empty tart. Top with an even layer of granola and bake until the filling begins to bubble, while being careful not to burn the granola, about 8-10 minutes. Remove the tart from the oven and allow to cool slightly before slicing. Top with ice cream and serve immediately.

TOMATO & RICOTTA GELATI WITH BASIL SEED PUDDING

"Gelati" in Philly parlance doesn't mean the plural of Italian gelato. Gelati is its own creature, allegedly invented at Italiano's in South Philly by layering water ice (page 154) and soft-serve like a sweetwise parfait. The local treat inspired this dessert from Rob Toland, pastry chef at Terrain, whose go-to at Rita's Water Ice is a mango/vanilla gelati. His restaurant version is a little more sophisticated, with ricotta ice cream and tomato granita, "somewhere between a dessert and a cheese course."

(SERVES 10)

For the ice cream:

3 cups whole milk

2½ cups granulated sugar, divided

1 cup whole-milk ricotta

12 large egg yolks

1 tablespoon vanilla extract

For the granita:

1 cup water

¾ pound Roma tomatoes, cored and quartered

½ pound strawberries, cored

½ teaspoon Diamond Crystal kosher salt

For the basil pudding:

¼ cup basil seeds (substitute chia seeds)

1 cup simple syrup

Fresh basil leaves, for garnish

To prepare the ice cream: Add the milk, 1½ cups of the sugar, and yolks to a medium stainless-steel pot set over medium heat and bring to 160°F, whisking constantly to avoid scorching. Switch to a rubber or silicone spatula and continue to stir and scrape the bottom of the pot until the mixture reaches 180°F. Strain the ice cream base into a blender and the ricotta in thirds, blending between each addition until fully incorporated. Strain the base into an airtight container and chill for at least 12 hours. Process the base in an ice cream maker according to the manufacturer's instructions and reserve frozen until ready to serve.

To prepare the granita: Combine the remaining sugar and the water in a sauce pot. Warm the mixture over medium heat, stirring until the sugar is completely dissolved. Measure out 7 tablespoons of the syrup and add to a medium mixing bowl, reserving the remainder in the pot at room temperature for later in the recipe. Place tomatoes in a blender

© HILARY MYERS

and puree until smooth. Strain the puree through a fine-mesh strainer into the bowl with the simple syrup. Discard the pulp. Puree the strawberries until smooth and add the strawberry puree to the strained tomato liquid, along with the salt. Whisk the mixture together to form the granita base and transfer to a shallow pan. Freeze the base, stirring and scraping with a fork every hour to create small, even ice crystals.

To prepare the pudding: While the granita is nearly done freezing, remove the ice cream from the freezer to soften for plating and make the basil pudding. Reheat the simple syrup and add the basil seeds to a small airtight container. Pour 1 cup of the warm syrup over the seeds. As the mixture cools, it will thicken and take on a pudding like consistency.

To serve: Chill then set out 10 individual serving bowls. Place a dollop of pudding in the bottom of each bowl and top with a scoop of ice cream. Cover each portion with granita and garnish with torn basil leaves. Serve immediately.

INDEX

A

Alma de Cuba, 24
Amada, 93
Asian-Spiced Tuna Burger, 119

B

Barbuzzo, 9
beef
  Beef Lettuce Cups with Tomato Salad, 14
  Cote de Boeuf for Two with Basquaise
    Panzanella, 142
  Roquefort-Stuffed Burger, 96
  Stout-Braised Short Ribs with Maitake
    Mushrooms, 104
Beef Lettuce Cups with Tomato Salad, 14
Bibb & Endive Salad, 42
Bibou, 117
Bistrot a La Minette, 21
Blackberry Elderflower Tart with Lemon Poppy
  Ice Cream, 162
Booker's Restaurant & Bar, 123
Bruschetta with Stracciatella & Fava Beans, 10
Buddakan, 69

C

Carbonara al Profumo di Tartufo Bianco e
  Acciughe, 74
Carrot-Pecan Cake with Maple-Cream Cheese
  Icing, 151
cheeses, local, 51
Cheesecake with Cajeta Caramel, 155
cheesesteak, 88
chicken
  Chicken Freekeh, 90
  Chicken Long Rice with Scallions and Crispy
    Chicken Skin, 55
  Chicken Mole Tortas, 139
  Chicken Pot Pie, 99

  Chicken Sausage, Egg & Cheese Breakfast Sand-
    wiches, 127
  Fried Jerk Chicken & Waffles with Pineapple
    Butter, 123
Chicken Freekeh, 90
Chicken Long Rice with Scallions and Crispy
  Chicken Skin, 55
Chicken Mole Tortas, 139
Chicken Pot Pie, 99
Chicken Sausage, Egg & Cheese Breakfast
  Sandwiches, 127
Chile en Nogada, 87
Chilled Cucumber-Avocado Soup with Smoked
  Pumpkin Seeds, 36
Cote de Boeuf for Two with Basquaise
  Panzanella, 142

D

Dan Dan Noodles, 77
Dandelion, The, 109
Death Rides a Pale Horse, 158
desserts
  Blackberry Elderflower Tart with Lemon Poppy
    Ice Cream, 162
  Carrot-Pecan Cake with Maple-Cream Cheese
    Icing, 151
  Cheesecake with Cajeta Caramel, 155
  Death Rides a Pale Horse, 158
  Hot Fudge Sundae, 148
  Rose & Pistachio Cruller, 159
  Tomato & Ricotta Gelati with Basil Seed
    Pudding, 165
Distrito, 17
drinks
  Blanc & Blue Martini, 41
  Death Rides a Pale Horse, 158

E

Edamame Ravioli, 69

eggs
    Chicken Sausage, Egg & Cheese Breakfast
      Sandwiches, 127
    Potato Gnocchi with Mushrooms & Egg, 72
    Salade Lyonnaise, 46
    Smoked Salmon Eggs Benedict with Home
      Fries, 112
    Uni with Warm Scrambled Eggs & Whipped
      Yogurt, 31
    Yellow Curry with Egg & Tofu, 131
El Rey, 85
Empanada de Verde with Onion Confit & Artichoke
  Escabeche, 24
entrees
    Asian-Spiced Tuna Burger, 119
    Chicken Freekeh, 90
    Chicken Mole Tortas, 139
    Chicken Pot Pie, 99
    Chicken Sausage, Egg & Cheese Breakfast
      Sandwiches, 127
    Chile en Nogada, 87
    Cote de Boeuf for Two with Basquaise
      Panzanella, 142
    Fried Jerk Chicken & Waffles with Pineapple
      Butter, 123
    Fish & Chips with Tartar Sauce, 109
    Lasagna Bolognese, 107
    Lechon Kawali with Garlic Fried Rice and Tomato
      Salad, 136
    Paella Valenciana, 93
    Pork Milanese with Arugula Salad, 84
    Pumpkin Pancakes, 115
    Roasted Duck with Potato Crique &
      Asparagus, 117
    Roquefort-Stuffed Burger, 96
    Smoked Salmon Eggs Benedict with Home
      Fries, 112
    Stout-Braised Short Ribs with Maitake
      Mushrooms, 104
    Whole Roasted Lamb Shoulder with
      Pomegranate, 91
    Yellow Curry with Egg & Tofu, 131

F
Fish & Chips with Tartar Sauce, 109
Fork, 58
Franklin Fountain, 148
Franklin Mortgage & Investment Co, The, 158
Fried Jerk Chicken & Waffles with Pineapple
  Butter, 123
Friday Saturday Sunday, 3

G
Gnocculi all'Argentiera, 62
Good Dog Bar, 96
Grilled Asparagus Salad, 49

H
Han Dynasty, 77
Hardena, 131
Hearts of Palm, Beach Style, 37
Honey's Sit N Eat, 151
Hot Fudge Sundae, 148
Hungry Pigeon, 127

I
In the Valley, 27

K
Kale & Feta Borekas, 6
Kanella, 52
K'Far, 5

L
Lalo, 135
Lasagna Bolognese, 107
Lechon Kawali with Garlic Fried Rice and Tomato
  Salad, 136
Lolita, 155

M
Melograno, 74
Metropolitan Bakery, 12
Morimoto, 66

N

N. 3rd, 119
New England Clam Chowder, 40

O

Oeuf du Pecheur, 21
Osteria, 82
Oyster House, 39
Oyster Stew, 39
Oysters with Frozen Meyer Lemon Mignonette, 3

P

Paella Valenciana, 93
Paesano's Philly Style, 107
Parc, 45
pastas
    Carbonara al Profumo di Tartufo Bianco e
        Acciughe, 74
    Dan Dan Noodles, 77
    Edamame Ravioli, 69
    Gnocculi all' Argentiera, 62
    Potato Gnocchi with Mushrooms & Egg, 72
    Soba Carbonara, 67
    Spaghetti with Green Tomatoes &
        Razor Clams, 63
    Suckling Pork Tortellini, 59
    Testaroli al Pesto di Asparagi, 76
Philly Pretzels, 19
pizza, 144
Poi Dog, 54
pork
    Lechon Kawali with Garlic Fried Rice and
        Tomato Salad, 136
    Pork Milanese with Arugula Salad, 84
    Suckling Pork Tortellini, 59
Pork Milanese with Arugula Salad, 84
Potato Gnocchi with Mushrooms & Egg, 72
Pumpkin, 103
Pumpkin Pancakes, 115

R

rice
    Chicken Long Rice with Scallions and Crispy
        Chicken Skin, 55

Lechon Kawali with Garlic Fried Rice, 136
    Paella Valenciana, 93
Roasted Duck with Potato Crique & Asparagus, 117
Rose & Pistachio Cruller, 159
Roquefort-Stuffed Burger, 96
Rouge, 42

S

Sabrina's Café, 112
Salade Lyonnaise, 46
salads
    Arugula Salad (with Pork Milanese), 84
    Bibb & Endive Salad, 42
    Grilled Asparagus Salad, 49
    Radish and Citrus Salad, 13
    Salade Lyonnaise, 46
    Watermelon Salad with Feta & Almonds, 52
Sampan, 13
seafood
    Asian-Spiced Tuna Burger, 119
    Carbonara al Profumo di Tartufo Bianco e
        Acciughe, 74
    Fish & Chips with Tartar Sauce, 109
    New England Clam Chowder, 40
    Oeuf du Pecheur, 21
    Oyster Stew, 39
    Oysters with Frozen Meyer Lemon Mignonette, 3
    Paella Valenciana, 93
    Smoked Salmon Eggs Benedict with Home
        Fries, 112
    Smoked Trout Mousse on Pumpernickel
        Toast, 27
    Soba Carbonara, 67
    Spaghetti with Green Tomatoes &
        Razor Clams, 63
    Sweet Shrimp with Radish & Citrus Salad, 13
    Uni with Warm Scrambled Eggs & Whipped
        Yogurt, 31
    Veracruz Ceviche, 17
    Watermelon Salad with Feta & Almonds, 52
Smoked Salmon Eggs Benedict with Home Fries, 112
Smoked Trout Mousse on Pumpernickel Toast, 27
Soba Carbonara, 67

soups
  Chicken Long Rice with Scallions and Crispy
    Chicken Skin, 55
  Chilled Cucumber-Avocado Soup with Smoked
    Pumpkin Seeds, 36
  Hearts of Palm, Beach Style, 37
  New England Clam Chowder, 40
  Oyster Stew, 39
South Philly Barbacoa, 138
Spaghetti with Green Tomatoes & Razor Clams, 63
Standard Tap, 99
starters & snacks
  Beef Lettuce Cups with Tomato Salad, 14
  Bruschetta with Stracciatella & Fava Beans, 11
  Empanada de Verde with Onion Confit &
    Artichoke Escabeche, 24
  Kale & Feta Borekas, 6
  Oeuf de Pecheur, 21
  Oysters with Frozen Meyer Lemon Mignonette, 3
  Smoked Trout Mousse on Pumpernickel
    Toast, 27
  Sweet Shrimp with Radish & Citrus Salad, 13
  Uni with Warm Scrambled Eggs & Whipped
    Yogurt, 31
  Veracruz Ceviche, 17
  Whipped Ricotta with Grilled French Table
    Bread, 10
Stout-Braised Short Ribs with Maitake
  Mushrooms, 104
Suckling Pork Tortellini, 59
Suraya, 159
Sweet Shrimp with Radish & Citrus Salad, 13

T
Talula's Garden, 71
Terrain Garden Cafe, 162
Testaroli al Pesto di Asparagi, 76
Tomato & Ricotta Gelati with Basil Seed
  Pudding, 165
Townsend, 141
Tria, 49

U
Uni with Warm Scrambled Eggs & Whipped
  Yogurt, 31

V
Vedge, 36
Veracruz Ceviche, 17
Vernick Food & Drink, 31
Vetri, 63

W
Watermelon Salad with Feta & Almonds, 52
water ice, 154
Whipped Ricotta with Grilled French Table
  Bread, 10
Whole Roasted Lamb Shoulder with
  Pomegranate, 91

Y
Yellow Curry with Egg & Tofu, 131

Z
Zahav, 89
Zeppoli, 61

Adam Erace is freelance writer contributing to *Men's Journal, Fortune, Travel+Leisure*, and more than 50 other publications. His writing has been recognized with awards from the International Association of Culinary Professionals and the Association of Food Journalists and he is the co-author of *Laurel: Modern American Flavors in Philadelphia* and *Dinner at the Club: 100 Years of Stories and Recipes from South Philly's Palizzi Social Club*. He lives in South Philly with his wife, Charlotte, and two maniacal rescue dogs, Lupo and Marco.

© NEAL SANTOS

© SUSAN YOUNG

April White is an award-winning food writer and recipe developer. She is the author of several books, including *Latin Evolution,* the debut cookbook of Iron Chef Jose Garces.

White is the former food editor of *Philadelphia* magazine, and her writing has also appeared in *Food & Wine, Every Day with Rachael Ray,* and *US Airways* magazine, among other publications. She lives in Philadelphia.